Rooftop

Architecture

Rooftop

Architecture

The Art of Going Through the Roof

AKIKO BUSCH

Henry Holt and Company
New York

A Read/Write Publication
First published in New York by Henry Holt and Company, Inc.

Published by Henry Holt and Company, Inc., 115 West 18th Street, New York, New York 10011.
Published in Canada by Fitzhenry & Whiteside Limited, 195 Allstate Parkway, Markham, Ontario L3R 4T8.

Library of Congress Cataloging-in-Publication Data

Busch, Akiko.
  Rooftop architecture : the art of going through the roof /
  by Akiko Busch.—1st ed.
      p.   cm.
  1. Buildings—Additions.   I. Title.
TH4816.2.B87   1991
7 2 1—d c 2 0   90-45482
  ISBN 0-8050-1179-X   CIP

Henry Holt books are available at special discounts for bulk purchases for sales promotions,
premiums, fund-raising, or educational use. Special editions or book excerpts can also be
created to specification.
  For details contact:
  Special Sales Director
  Henry Holt and Company, Inc.
  115 West 18th Street
  New York, New York 10011

First Edition

Designed by Jennifer Place
Manufactured in Singapore
Recognizing the importance of preserving the written word, Henry Holt and Company, Inc.,
by policy, prints all of its first editions on acid-free paper.
10 9 8 7 6 5 4 3 2 1

To Brian

Acknowledgments

Rooftop Architecture originated as an article that was published in *Metropolis* magazine in the Fall of 1984, and for that reason I am grateful to Lee Ryder, then editor of the magazine and to Horace Havemeyer III, its publisher. Their support and interest in the subject encouraged the early research into what became this book. Susan Szenasy, the current editor of the magazine, has also been characteristically generous with advice, contacts, archives of information, and of course, phone numbers. As a contributing editor of the magazine, I am indebted to it—both for providing a forum for the early article and for its ongoing support for the project over the years

Since the publication of the article, I have spoken to innumerable architects, designers, and planners who have confessed their own longings to "go through the roof." Although many of them have not yet found a practical way to do so, their interest—indeed fascination—with rooftop acreage was continuing reassurance that the rooftop is an urban frontier waiting to be explored.

I am most grateful, though, to all of those who have gone through the roof successfully and to their partners who have documented the trip. Their invigorating accounts, verbal and illustrative, are the basis both for this book and, with any luck, for the future rooftop investigations that will be made by other urban dwellers. Although a complete list of these contributors is too lengthy to include here, I am especially thankful to those whose accounts included not only photographs, drawings, elevations, and floor plans, but the more philosophical musings that rooftop architecture seems so naturally to engender. These generous contributors include Caroll Michels, Lee Skolnick, Peter Wheelwright, Henry Smith-Miller, Jane Siris, Peter Coombs, Karen Jacobson, Andy Bartle, Jenny Shakespeare, and Phillip Smith.

I am indebted as well to the photographers who have so generously made their work available to me. Particularly helpful were Dick Busher, Karen Bussolini, Christopher Irion, Elliott Kaufman, Norman McGrath, Robert Perron, Erica Stoller, Tim Street-Porter, and Paul Warchol.

Finally, I thank Barbara Fishman for her thoughtful editing of the manuscript and Jennifer Place for her vision and skill in the design of this book. My gratitude is extended as well to Dorothy Spencer at Read/Write Press, to Ellen Greene, and to Marian Wood at Henry Holt and Company for guiding this book through production, as laborious a task certainly, as going through the roof and one that at times evoked other meanings of that phrase.
My thanks.

CONTENTS

Introduction:
The Eccentricities of the Roofline

We define our cities in innumerable ways—as business, financial, and industrial centers and as resources for culture, art, fashion. Individual streets, buildings, plazas, the color and texture of building facades, the quality of light, the proximity of mountains or sea are all the ingredients that compose our more personal, sensory impressions and perceptions of these places. Yet often it is the profile of the urban skyline that lodges itself most securely in our imagination; the varied and vibrant lexicon of roofline shapes that most clearly and definitively identifies individual cities.

In New York, it was once the Woolworth and Chrysler buildings that were the skyline landmarks; today, it is the towers of the World Trade Center, the slant of Citicorp Center, and the Chippendale pediment of the AT&T headquarters that have practically become symbols of the city itself. In Chicago, it is the Sears Tower. In San Francisco, the TransAmerica Pyramid and the tower of

the Bank of America serve the same purpose. In London, it is the dome of St. Paul's Cathedral. Indeed, it is by their rooflines that these buildings, indeed whole cities, are etched not only into the skyline, but into our collective imagination and memory as well.

The prominence of the skyline is not surprising when we take into account the fact that the skyscraper is the foremost building form of the twentieth century. What occurs at the skyline can be a sign of corporate prowess, miraculous feats of engineering and technology, sheer ornamental delight, or a combination of these elements. Often, the message of these architectural trajectories is one of corporate one-upmanship. That height confers status is a fact known to every schoolchild, and it has remained a fact of no small significance to the business magnates—and their architects—of recent history. Rooftop ornamentation has served such ends with admirable decorative, if not moral, certainty even in the early days of the skyscraper. In a lively discussion of New York City's downtown publishing district in the late nineteenth century, Michele Herman likens the changing roofline of the various newspapers' headquarters to the abrupt scene changes in a play. The headquarters for *The New York Times* were made significantly taller with

the removal of the gabled and mansarded roofs and their replacement by extra floors for offices. The headquarters for the nearby *Tribune,* meanwhile, removed its own tower, inserted its own extra floors, and then replaced the tower. (Michele Herman, "The Fourth Estate's Former Home," *Metropolis,* March 1990, p. 74)

The roofscape invites, even encourages, such antics; indeed, it is a landscape of the fantastic. And fortunately, for the most part the domes, cupolas, steeples, spires, and pyramids, and the infinity of decorative deviations on the essential formats that crown otherwise austere office buildings are motivated less by ambition than by the way they engage our imagination. There are environmental psychologists who would insist that the potency of these forms is in their sexual imagery; however, most of us can take pleasure in them for their pure, unrestrained ornamentalism. Urban critic Brendan Gill observes in his foreword to *Top of the City,* a book of photographs of New York's rooftop world compiled by Laura Rosen, "We look up, knowing that it is upon the tops of buildings that, generation after generation, the architects of the city have lavished their talents. It is there that they have given their so often hobbled imaginations full rein. In the late nineteenth century, the tops of the skyscrapers often took the shape of domes, surmounted by jaunty gilded lanterns; later came ziggurats, mausoleums, Alexandrian lighthouses, miniature Parthenons." (Laura Rosen, *Top of the City: New York's Hidden Rooftop World,* New York, New York, Thames & Hudson, 1982).

Happily, the eccentricity of these building forms is only matched by that of their occupants; The sandstone gargoyles, cupids and sirens, and the terra cotta knights and phoenixes emerging from their granite crevices make for a picturesque and ever-vigilant rooftop army, guardians of the more excitable creatures below.

In some cases, the reign of this rooftop army is an undeniable reign of terror. It was not unlikely for that master of the horrific, Steven King, to be asked to write the introduction to *Nightmares in the Sky,* a photographic investigation of gargoyles and grotesques in urban architecture. While King thought himself an unlikely candidate for the essay, the following conversation with the photographer, Marc Glimcher, changed his mind: "Then he (Glimcher) said something I'll never forget, something which not only convinced me to

Haus-Rucker's rooftop conservatory proposed for the Ansonia Hotel

9

write this essay, good or bad as it may be, but made it impossible not to write it. 'Because they are almost always above human sightlines, and because people in the city rarely look up, they don't see... *them*.' he said, gesturing to the horror across the street, the horror so strikingly at odds with the anonymous building from which sprang, like a tumor sprouting from the mild brow of some harmless, middle-aged and middle-class executive. 'But *they*... well, you'll notice that they're almost always looking down.' He paused, then smiled again. The smile was different this time: thoughtful, and I think, the tiniest bit uncomfortable." (f-stop Fitzgerald, *Nightmares in the Sky: Gargoyles and Grostesques,* New York, New York, Viking Studio Books, 1988, p. 9)

But in sync with the eccentric and often ominous spirit of grotesques and gargolyes are the rooftop forms with less predictable personas. Architects have not fashioned the eccentricities of the urban skyline alone; there are also those less intentionally ornamental and more random landmarks of the urban rooftop: Wooden water towers perched on slender stilts, trapezoidal skylights, stack pipes and vents, and spidery fire ladders are all poised on rooftops in their own random but sculptural arrangements. Even the elongated arms of construction cranes that loom above the skyscrapers they are in the process of building seem a natural ingredient of the eccentric urban skyline.

The silhouette of the rooftop has not escaped the notice of advertisers either; it is on rooftops that we encounter gigantic creatures in pursuits perhaps less heroic than those of their sandstone and granite colleagues—smoking huge cigarettes and drinking immense beers. There is also the three-dimensional variety of advertising, like the brightly colored Yale truck hoisted above New York's West 42nd Street, many feet above any thoroughfare it might actually be driven on. For years, one of Hoboken, New Jersey's favorite waterfront landmarks was the gigantic Maxwell House coffee cup tipped precariously over the roof of the factory on the bank of the Hudson River. And then there is the Campbell Soup Company's plant in Camden, New Jersey. On its rooftop, two water towers that more or less resemble the proportions of soup cans have been painted with the company's label; among other things these towers might bring to mind are the calamitous floods of tomato soup that might swamp the streets of Camden should the water towers ever be ruptured.

While the public location and grand scale of

city buildings themselves have often invited advertisers to hawk their wares on the visible facades of buildings, the very height and rooftop profile of individual buildings have urged the imagagination to new limits. For many years, a building at Eighth Avenue and 34th Street in New York City, with a wedding cake setback on its upper floors, advertised Winston filter cigarettes. The individual cigarettes emerged from the packet to coordinate ingeniously with the setbacks of the building.

If the rooftop terrain unleashes the imagination, it is no surprise that some of the architectural ventures on it are more private. The splendors of the rooftop are not all intended for public viewing. Indeed, there is a more private rooftop world where a lucky few have always taken up solitary, and sometimes splendid, residence.

Living at the top has an odd history. Its lineage is not so splendid. Most New York City penthouses were originally constructed as housing for

servants, and rooftop rooms were often added haphazardly as one's domestic staff grew. Even in these earlier days, however, eccentricities marked rooftop buildings. Consider New York City's elegant Ansonia Hotel, the highly decorated beaux arts building with an extravagant collection of turrets, gables, balconies, and arches. It is not exactly the ideal location for a working farm, but that is exactly what it was for a short period of time immediately after it was constructed in 1902. Built by W.E.D. Stokes, the hotel accommodated permanent residents as well as guests. Among the not-so-glamorous roster of the latter were a flock of chickens, some sheep, and, allegedly, a cow on its rooftop, which Stokes had apparently converted to a veritable pasture. Stokes's motivation for establishing a barnyard on his roof is not entirely clear, as he also possessed a country estate in the Berkshire Mountains. Nevertheless, until the inevitable intervention of the Health Department, Stokes' rooftop farm thrived.

Although penthouses may originally have been intended as housing for the hired help, they didn't keep that function for long. As urban density increased, luxury, wealth, and status could be demonstrated by having the means to achieve privacy and solitude. The penthouse, of course, is one such logical means, and it soon became synonymous with luxury. The social exile these rooftop quarters once signified was replaced with a more enviable sense of solitude. Early penthouses were often, ironically, simply refurbished maids' quarters. Or, once apartment buildings began to be designed intentionally with high-rent penthouses, these might be formed by a series of setbacks that make for ample views and terraces, if not especially inventive architecture.

Haus-Rucker's proposal of Mediterranean Rooftop Gardens for a series of row houses

Today, privacy and space being ever rarer urban commodities, the most extravagant penthouses are perhaps those in which the altitude itself signals the degree of luxury. Apartments and penthouses have achieved new heights, quite literally, in such new residential and mixed-use urban towers as Chicago's 100-story John Hancock Tower and New York City's 68-story Trump Tower, 78-story Metropolitan Tower, and 75-story Cityspire. The decor of such apartments is usually preordained by their peculiar altitude, with beds, couches, and desks that are positioned for the view and with mirrors and other glass and metal surfaces that reflect it.

Slightly closer to earth in the stratosphere are new apartments built atop buildings that were "underbuilt." With urban air rights becoming nearly as precious a commodity as the building lots themselves, enterprising developers are refining their skills at making money out of thin air. Air rights, the unused space above or around a building, are a legal commodity that can often be sold or transferred within a city block. Depending on local zoning ordinances, existing buildings can combine their own unused air space with that purchased from adjacent buildings to have whole floors—indeed whole floors of luxury apartments and penthouses—added on to them. And with apartments and condominiums at higher floor levels commanding higher prices, the appeal of such development is obvious, not only to urban developers but also to co-op boards looking to lower their monthly maintenance fees.

Living at the top can indeed be a question of glamour when the apartment floats somewhere over fifty stories. And it can be a question of entrepreneurial marketing and development when a low building becomes a tall one. But more interesting, more provocative and in the end more exotic are rooftop dwellings that, while aspiring to slightly lower altitudes, easily achieve greater heights of the imagination.

For many young architects, especially urban architects, the chances to design and build on a vacant building lot are few. Their commissions are usually earned by renovating and restructuring existing spaces. Although the demands of such jobs may be no less than those of new construction, most young architects reach a point in their careers when the prospects of new construction are irresistible and inevitable. For many of

Below and Right *Haus-Rucker's rooftop proposal for the American Indian Museum*

them, the rooftop may be the only vacant building lot. For them as well as for willing urban homesteaders, the rooftop is the new frontier.

In the early seventies an experimental non-profit urban design group known as Haus-Rucker Inc. received a research grant from the National Endowment for the Arts to investigate alternative uses of the urban rooftop. To date, their work may be the most comprehensive study on the subject. And although their findings remain written rather than built, the research suggests new ways in which public and private rooftops can be put to greater use to serve recreational, educational, and commercial, as well as residential, ends.

The group selected New York City as its study site—applying the universal and cross-cultural logic that asserts that if you can do it in New York, you can do it anywhere. (In fact, the city's building codes are so stringent that that logic is probably valid.) Also, there are approximately twenty thousand acres of the urban outdoors on New York City's rooftops, or twenty-three times the acreage found in Central Park. Using the image of the rooftop oasis, the study addressed issues of the historical and sociological aspects of rooftop development; building codes; safety and security measures; flooring surfaces; shelters and enclosures; wind and sun screens; illumination systems; and the potential for botanical and agricultural life on the rooftop. As part of its practical guide for recycling rooftops, the group also advised prospective rooftop tenants on how to learn about city building laws; zoning regulations; fire districts; liability laws; and how to determine whether a particular rooftop is a viable building site. The focus of the research was not simply on how individual tenants might make use of the urban rooftop but on how the rooftop might be adapted to serve a broader public in a more comprehensive, humanistic strategy for urban and planning. As the group stated in its guidebook:

"Would it [the recycling of the city rooftop] not provide a great psychological lift for those of us who were raised to believe that the American Dream entitles every citizen to a back yard, although we find ourselves living within the boundaries of a balcony rail or apartment door!

This is not to suggest that rooftop space should be subdivided into rigid, private plots in the lethally monotonous suburban pattern. But if rooftop space were considered the 'urban back yard,' our yearning for a way of life well balanced between the dynamics of the city and enjoyment in the outdoors could well be satisfied.

While recycled rooftop space is not the urban cure-all, a marriage of the city's cultural, recreational, educational, and business resources with a new approach to rooftop use has a future far greater than anyone can predict. Comprehensive rooftop development can create new jobs and new professions; it can generate revenue for the city and/or private enterprise; and it can create incentives to keep people in the city and lure back expatriots."

(Hans-Rucker Inc., *Rooftop Oasis Project: Tenant's Guide to Organizing a Rooftop Project,* edited by Caroll Michels, New York, 1976, p. 1.)

To complement the practical information gathered, the group also developed prototypes for its study. The group devised alternate rooftop utilization programs for a variety of different urban building types, including a museum, row houses, an office building, a hotel, a school, a hospital, and a department store. These programs were more exotic exercises of the imagination. "By the Light of the Silvery Moon" was the name given to the glass conservatory proposed for the rooftop of the Ansonia Hotel. A far cry from the barnyard that once occupied the roof, this more elegant conservatory was to be equipped with a bar and a restaurant and was to include year-round climate control for the indoor tropical plant life. Plans for the outdoors specified a formal outdoor promenade and park, ornamented with "living arches," actually sculptured shrubs that would make for more intimate "sitting nests."

The proposal for the Museum of the American Indian was developed on the assumption that the museum needed both to expand its interior exhibition space and to create an area for outdoor exhibitions and demonstrations. A platform was designed to be constructed over the existing roof as a stage for special events and temporary exhibitions. A Pueblo village was to be reconstructed on a space-frame construction extending from the ground level to the platform, and the interior of the space frame was to accommodate an auditorium. The plan went so far as to specify that the facade of an adjacent apartment building be painted as a mountain "to enhance the simulated village's natural setting."

Drawing on different ethnic resources, the group proposed Mediterranean rooftop gardens for a series of eighteenth-century row houses. The proposal capitalized on the existing 'furniture' of the rooftop—shafts, bulkheads, parapets, and even the level changes—to "create a unified landscape, giving residents access to one large space instead of confining them to only the roof over the build-ing. The roofscape provides community gathering areas, unstructured and free spaces for 'backyard' activities, as well as secluded niches when privacy is desired."

These are only some of the varied rooftop agendas devised by Haus-Rucker and they indeed make for a grand reuse strategy. Designed for public use and oriented toward entire urban communities, they may be the civic-minded design plans so urgently needed in many inner cities. These are projects that look for the participation both of individuals and of the business and municipal communities. Still, their grand scale may be just what has prevented them from being implemented.

All the same, architects and urban homesteaders alike are recognizing that the rooftop is terrain ripe for development. In New York, as well as in other metropolitan areas where urban density has made housing scarce and costly, rooftop building is increasingly seen as a viable option. And although the physical proportions of rooftop constructions may be on a smaller scale than that possible for construction on the ground level, the wit, imagination, and overall inventiveness these structures introduce as strategies for relevant urban design are no less than those of the Haus-Rucker proposals.

The rooftop—currently the conventional residence for water tanks and air-conditioning and elevator equipment—is gradually being reclaimed for human tenants. If urban density is provoking an urban exodus from some cities, then this "vertical edge" may become all the more relevent as a place simply to get more space. The virgin acreage of the rooftop is inviting to architects not simply as the site on which to unleash their fantasies, but as a practical building lot for residential, and sometimes even commercial, applications. Addressing congestion, lack of privacy, and cramped living quarters, the rooftop can offer pragmatic solutions to problems of urban housing. Rooftop construction can also be a part of an overall recycling agenda for urban preservation. That services—heating, wiring, sewerage and water lines—have all been previously installed only a few feet below can make the rooftop site all the more expedient from the outset.

The rooftops themselves vary from those of three-story brownstones to industrial warehouses to thirty-story apartment buildings. Occasionally, rooftop additions acknowledge the style or the

Haus-Rucker's rooftop proposal for a department store

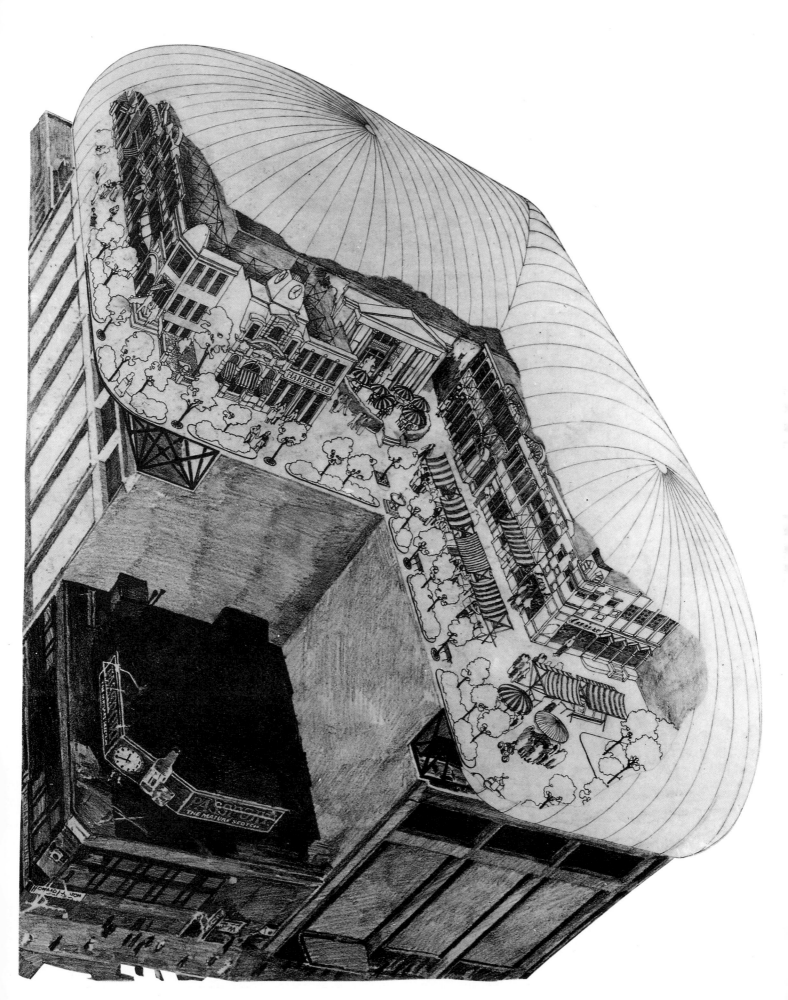

facade of the existing building. And some adhere to the materials of the rooftop vernacular of tar paper and corrugated tin. For the most part, however, they deviate more imaginatively with clapboard and shingles and plaster and stucco and glass. While these habitats invariably address the practicalities of everyday living, they may also astonish us, and in the end it may be that element of surprise that links them together.

Building at the rooftop implies basic changes in how we see things. Stylistically, what evolves on the rooftop tends to be mysterious, provocative, inventive. Architect Lee Skolnick points out that a basic perceptual reversal—between what is above and what is below ground—occurs when one builds on the roof. While maintaining the grid of the urban landscape, the roofscape floats and hovers, receding into canyons and crevices before climbing again to assorted heights. On the landscape of the rooftop, architecture is connected more to space and sky than it is to the street. There is a sense of distance, and often tranquility. The sense of solitude that is granted to the rural dweller by geography is suggested here simply by height. There is an undeniable element of escape. Rooftops occupy a remote territory that is physically and psychologically removed from the urban turmoil below.

And it is exactly this sense of distance that is so liberating to architects of the rooftop. Less restricted by the grid of the street facades of adjacent buildings, rooftop architecture has fewer aesthetic restrictions imposed on it than its earthbound cousins. Rooftop constructions may observe to varying degress the larger structures of their terrain—the slopes, plains, and towers of their surroundings—as well as the smaller peculiarities of their landscape—the skylights, air shafts, and water towers, to name only a few. But there are no pre-established aesthetics of the rooftop, and indeed, it is an almost metaphorical terrain of stylistic freedom for many urban architects.

Despite the innate practicality of building on the rooftop, the aesthetics of rooftop architecture are unlikely to make for a marriage of convenience; rather, the union between a rooftop addition and the existing building may resemble those second marriages where the age gap between the two partners is not the least factor in the great incompatibility of the match; those marriages in which style, appearance, and personal history or lack thereof, all seem to be at odds, doing nothing whatever to suggest compatibility between the partners. And it is exactly this profound incompatibility that in the end delights the marriage partners, their friends, and their detractors and makes the marriage a lasting one. Consider the water tower that graced the roofline of the Federal Screw and Supply Building in New York's lower Manhattan in the early 1980s: It was wrapped in gold lame parachute material. That this rooftop exhibition was only temporary suggests an ecstatic weekend fling more than it does a solid marriage; all the same, it was the utter incongruity of materials that so delighted passersby.

Ordinary human capriciousness loves incongruity, be it between marriage partners or building styles. Like English garden follies, possibly their only known stylistic precedent, rooftop

Haus-Rucker's rooftop proposal for the American Indian Museum

habitats feature the unpredictable. As a child living in Detroit, filmmaker Peter Hutton became fascinated by the water towers of New York City when he saw a Charles Addams cartoon in *The New Yorker* picturing a milk bottle mysteriously poised outside a rooftop water tower. Childhood fantasies having the psychological potency that they do, the image followed him, and when he later became a resident of New York City, it was his fervent desire to take up residence in a water tower. Hutton went so far as to design his home as a series of interconnected water towers, with mechanical roofs that might open to the sky, somewhat as the lens of a camera opens to the light. Sadly, Hutton's plans were never realized: The manufacturers of water towers found Hutton's notion more comic than practical, and the voracious financial appetite of his films took swift care of his financing. Although Hutton's village of water towers was never realized, many other equally fanciful structures have indeed been constructed.

For reasons altogether different than those of the manicured English garden, the zone of the roof invites, even encourages, eccentricity. In ages past, lighthouses and ziggurats might be found there. Contemporary rooftops invite the same eccentricity; despite the practicality of the rooftop building lot, one is apt to find there pristine glassed-in libraries, skyrooms, serene Japanese pools, and tranquil Greek temples. Clearly, this is terrain where pragmatism and eccentricity go hand in hand. Indeed, the ability with which many architects are going through the roof suggests not the calamity traditionally associated with this act, but rather, the arrival of a new building form.

Because rooftops are an open invitation to invention, it is often difficult to catalogue their styles. Certainly some can be classified by their materials or by already established architectural styles. But more often, these habitats defy classification—a problem for no one, of course, except the finicky writer or editor. That being the case here, I have tried to organize these eccentric habitats under logical chapter headings— realizing all the while that doing so is a questionable enterprise, the rooftop being a terrain where such conventional logic is often happily absent.

All drawings courtesy of Haus-Rucker-Inc., Rooftop Oasis Project; *Tenant's Guide to Organizing A Rooftop Project,* edited by Caroll Michels, New York, 1976.

URBAN COTTAGES:

The Sheds, Shanties, Cabins, Pavilions, and Throne Rooms of Tar Beach

Introduction

Calling the rooftop zone "the second city in the sky," as it has been dubbed, is only slightly inaccurate. For the moment, at least, it remains a village rather than a city. All the same, the tone of the metaphor rings true, natural even. Given the surrounding urban congestion and the innate human appetite for things heavenly, it should come as no surprise that a second city be constructed sky high.

As one might expect, rooftop constructions are every bit as diverse as those built on the ground. The case could be made that they even exhibit greater stylistic freedom. Even the most cursory glance will discover that rooftop constructions tend to demonstrate a freewheeling style. Their design inevitably seems to be a little less restrained, a little more on the wild side.

Indeed, the extreme design strategies we confront on the rooftop are the calculated responses to the extreme conditions of the rooftop. Foremost of these are the physical conditions. Urban rooftop architecture must be pragmatic. The structural integrity of a rooftop addition must be such that it can stand up to severe weather conditions, heavy wind loads, stringent fire regulations, and the ever-looming threat of leaking on the tenants below.

Beyond the physical conditions are the aesthetic conditions—or lack of them—that also factor into rooftop design. The rooftop provides a building lot with few visual or aesthetic connections to the building below. In some cases, architects of the rooftop *do* look to the base building or to other buildings in the immediate neighborhood for their design cues. Theodore Brown has designed a discreet rooftop addition for a three-story building in San Francisco that takes its visual directives from the bay windows of the existing building. But for the most part, architects and designers of the rooftop are less likely than their earthbound colleagues to look to the immediate site for design directives. One rooftop addition designed by architects Peter Coombs and Jane Siris not only deviates in its style from the building below but even is oriented in an entirely different direction—facing a river view to the west instead of facing north to the street. Invariably, the rooftop becomes a metaphor; it is symbolic territory for architects and builders for whom the sky may be the limit.

The most important common goal in the design of rooftop cottages may be privacy, a sense of seclusion not only from the city at large, but from the more immediate neighbors who may even share the rooftop. The different ways in which this privacy can be claimed may be what lies behind the great diversity of rooftop design. We associate rooftop architecture with expansive vistas of the city skyscape; and indeed, many such additions address these views while nevertheless achieving a sense of solitude. But not all rooftops have sensational views, and it is often the intent of the architect to carve a more private retreat, one that remains hidden and secluded. Architect Peter Wheelwright has gone so far as to design a rooftop addition that accommodates both sensibilities.

Going through the roof is a pragmatic way to create more space in crowded urban areas. Rooftop constructions are built primarily to create new living spaces or to expand existing small ones. But they are also polemic exercises in which urban architects are given the rare chance to test ideas that might be less appropriate on the ground. Rooftops are indeed open acreage, literally and figuratively; they allow architects not simply to build functional cabins, cottages and aerie pavilions but also to investigate form and fantasy in a zone with fewer aesthetic or stylistic restrictions than those binding builders on the ground.

Overleaf *Siris/Coombs residence, exterior view*

Left *Rooftop pavilion, Paris, France*

A Modernist Silo
New York, New York

I. M. Pei
New York, New York

As a real estate developer, entrepreneur, and often flamboyant urban visionary, William Zeckendorf built his reputation on real estate gambles that almost always paid off. Given his flair for the dramatic, it is no surprise that Zeckendorf was drawn to the theatrical in architecture. And with a keen intuition with respect to urban real estate, it also comes as no surprise that he looked to the rooftop in the early fifties—decades earlier than most other architects and developers—as a viable building plot. The rooftop of the twin Manhattan office towers housing Zeckendorf's firm of Webb & Knapp provided cheap, usable space that could be spacious and filled with natural light. More to the point, perhaps, was its crowning position above Madison Avenure, an appropriate location for the

tycoon to make his deals and observe the minuscule maneuverings of the earthlings below.

Architect I. M. Pei was then director of Webb & Knapp's architectural division. The two-story penthouse he designed for Zeckendorf was a modernist's investigation of small circular or cylindrical spaces floating inside larger rectangular spaces. The lower floor accommodates executive and ancillary offices, a reception area, a lounge, accounting and storage space, and, of course, Zeckendorf's private office.

Pei's dilemma was how to preserve a sense of openness and spaciousness for visitors and other employees while reserving for Zeckendorf the luxuries of the traditional corner office. His solution was a private office designed as a circular space that was pulled back into the reception area. As such, it is central and assertive as a magnate's office is destined to be. Its circular form and only slightly recessive position within the overall office did not prevent visitors from being impressed with

Left *Zeckendorf penthouse, exterior view*

Above *Zeckendorf penthouse, lobby*

the height and view of the rooftop aerie, most notably through the glass walls of the reception area that open onto the rooftop terrace and pool.

Zeckendorf's office is a twenty-five foot, teakwood cylinder with doors that open to the reception area and terrace. A glass transom running the length of its uppermost perimeter brings in light and opens the office visually, preventing it from feeling like an oversized tin can. Accoustical panels (described by some as resembling "standing coffins for Zeckendorf's competitors") have been installed around the perimeter of the room to deflect the awkward reverbations that occur in circular enclosures.

In designing lighting for the penthouse, Pei specified a system of skylights, augmented by exterior spotlights. Their light was then diffused through cylinders through the roof slab to the ceiling. The architect also accommodated Zeckendorf's taste for theatrics: the tycoon requested a system of "mood control," in which the intensity and color of light could be controlled by dimmers concealed in his desk. Although there is no documentation as to the effectiveness of this device in his business negotiations, one can only make conjectures about Zeckendorf and his possible ob-

servations and applications of the effects of illumination on the human psyche.

An elevator, installed in a freestanding cylinder outside Zeckendorf's office, leads to the crow's nest above, a second and larger freestanding cylindrical space. Here, in a more secluded and opulent aerie, is Zeckendorf's private dining room and entertainment area, equipped with kitchen, bar, and bath.

Photographs: Ezra Stoller, copyright © ESTO

Right   *View of Zeckendorf penthouse at night*

Below   *View of Zeckendorf private office*

Suburban Seclusion
New York, New York

Siris/Coombs Architects
New York, New York

When architects Jane Siris and Peter Coombs bought a $38,000 penthouse on the rooftop of a thirteen-story co-op building on Manhattan's Upper West Side, it wasn't with the plan of installing their family in the small, tin shanty/studio as it was. The 400-square-foot shed had leaks and drafts and was positioned partially beneath the building's water tank in an almost subversive siting. What they instead envisioned for their purchase was the installation of essential services— electricity, heat, and plumbing lines—and the roofrights for four hundred extra square feet of expansion. The bonus was the freight elevator that went directly to their new building lot.

Indeed, the fourteen hundred square foot residence they eventually replaced the studio with is

a three-story house with three terraces, a greenhouse, and even a gas barbecue—all far more suggestive of a suburban family house and backyard than they are of a city apartment. What gives the truth away, of course, is that the expansive views are not of their neighbors' garden, but of the grander city skyline and the Hudson River.

Devising this suburban illusion wasn't easy. The wind velocities at the level of the fourteenth floor as well as stringent fire codes persuaded the architects to use steel framing rather than wood. Which is where the elevator came in: Rather than hoisting the steel I-beams to the roof with a crane, they hauled them up by the freight elevator. But because the beams, at twenty-eight feet, were bigger than the elevator, they were cut down at ground level, and reassembled, or rather welded, on the rooftop's north terrace in what became a veritable rooftop steel yard.

One of the great attractions of living on the rooftop is the proximity one can have with the out-

---

Above *Siris/Coombs residence, steps separating kitchen and dining areas*

Left *Siris/Coombs addition, exterior view*

27

doors, a closeness to nature customarily reserved for rural dwellers. Such an intimacy with the outdoors, especially when enforced, may be less appealing to the construction crew of the rooftop building. Neither the crew nor the architects were able to anticipate all the problems such a site would pose. The weather conditions that have such a strong impact on any building site are all the more critical when the site is a rooftop. In this case, wind delayed the project considerably, as the crew would understandably hold off when the steel beams began to wave in strong gusts of wind blowing across the Hudson. In winter, snow disposal consisted of loading snow into wheelbarrows and transporting it to the section of the roof with proper drainage. And overall weatherproofing inevitably consisted of arranging plastic "tents" over areas of the house under construction.

With four-hundred square feet of available roofrights, the architects decided to build up to get all the space their family wanted. Indeed, the structure is decidedly vertical. Even the slanted roofline, a sort of residential-scale Citicorp pinnacle, allows just enough space for a top-floor, light-filled study. To visually reduce the building's height to a more domestic scale, the architects specified pink,

horizontal stucco bands at the different floor levels of the exterior.

To convey a feeling of spaciousness and light in the interior of what was a very vertical structure, the architects omitted interior walls where possible, changing the floor levels and materials instead to suggest different areas. The living room, for example, is set below the original roofline, a position that established a format for built-in banquette seating and the three, low steps that lead up the terrace. The kitchen has a formal eating and serving area with ash finishes and a preparation area slightly below it finished in plastic laminates. With skylights, large windows, and the entries from outdoor terraces, the outdoors is brought in. Such terraces provide city dwellers with a rare opportunity to expand their domestic landscape to the outdoors.

Below *Siris/Coombs residence, living area*

Above Right *Siris/Coombs residence, upper-level study*

Below Right *Siris/Coombs addition, exterior view*

A Pleasure Perch
New York, New York

Siris/Coombs Architects
New York, New York

Architect Jane Siris describes her client as "a bachelor looking for a pleasure palace." And as he also owned the top floor of the four-story, painted limestone building on Manhattan's Upper West Side, the obvious place to start looking for it was on the rooftop. As befitting contemporary standards of luxury, this pleasure palace—a perch, in fact, considering its site—was to include a hot tub and deck. Fortunately, the building faced south, the correct exposure for any bona fide pleasure palace.

The rooftop addition, about twenty by twenty-five feet, included a bedroom, a bath, closets, and stairs to the apartment below. Facing south, its windows and doors were positioned to absorb as much natural daylight as possible. The design also exploited the unusual pitch of the rooftop: Its steep drop toward the front of the building al-

lowed for decking to be installed around it, with the hot tub dropped into the decking, which itself would be flush with the edge of the roof.

The masonry and stucco cottage is surrounded by canyons of much taller apartment buildings; and despite two decorative horizontal pink bands, its style is austere—especially compared to the more ornamented facade of the building it rests on. Still, its design is hardly oblivious to the city around it. Most urban pleasure palaces are defined by their degree of insulation from the urban chaos that surrounds them; how well buffered they are from the public zone of the city is as important as the sensuality of their appointments. What is unique about this one, poised openly on the edge of the rooftop, is its happy recognition of—indeed, happy coexistence with—its urban surroundings.

Left and Above *Siris/Coombs addition, exterior construction views*

A Change of Face
New York, New York

Siris/Coombs Architects
New York, New York

The orientation of this rooftop in New York City's Greenwich Village was not especially inviting: The seven-story manufacturing building that had been converted to residential units faced north, and there was no hint of the Hudson River which was only a block away. What architect Jane Siris's clients, a professional couple, wanted was to increase the usable space of their duplex loft. Going through the roof was the obvious answer.

Using a boom crane, the architects added a third floor—a cottage—to the duplex. They broke through to the second floor of the duplex later by installing a staircase connecting the south-facing master bedroom with the cottage, which was to become the rooftop study. Although constructing a rooftop addition before making the interior con-

nection may not always be the most practical way to build, notes Siris, it is one way to avoid leaks.

Unlike many rooftop additions, this one did not share the orientation of the existing building. Rather, the architects found that by positioning the rooftop cottage to face west, they would gain both a river view and ample afternoon sunlight. And by installing a cedar deck in front of the addition, they were able to capitalize on both of these gains. Skylights puncturing the pitched roof of the cottage bring in additional light, and a section of glass block flooring in the new study draws this natural daylight from the rooftop level to the interior recesses of this now triplex home.

To further augment the usable space of the triplex, the architects designed a stepped deck for the second floor. Although the deck faces north, it too looks out over the river, with its hot tub being the most accommodating vantage point for this vista. A network of white pipe railing that includes a small ladder connects the upper and low-

---

Above *Siris/Coombs triplex, rooftop view*

Left *Private terrace of Siris/Coombs triplex*

er terraces. Used indoors as well in the study and staircase, the metal piping functions as a visual and functional link between the indoors and out.

With its odd assortment of stack vents, skylights, and other rooftop paraphernalia, this particular roofscape seems somewhat chaotic. And with its pitched roof, pink stucco facade, white trim, and flower boxes, the cottage seems more in sync with a country village than with the more aggressive urban landscapes of Greenwich Village. However, it is exactly this improbable design and placement of the cottage and its sunny terraces that create this tranquility. Which, after all, is just the purpose of most urban rooftop architecture.

Above Right   *Private deck of Siris/Coombs triplex*

Above Far Right   *Stairway leading to Siris/Coombs rooftop addition*

Below Far Right   *Tiered deck and hot tub of Siris/Coombs rooftop*

Below Left   *Siris/Coombs triplex, interior with glass block floor*

Below Right   *Siris/Coombs triplex, interior with skylight*

Bay View Extension
San Francisco, California

Theodore Brown & Partners, Inc.
San Francisco, California

In determining the design of a rooftop addition, architect Theodore Brown first considers the views from the site. This is understandable, considering that his practice is in San Francisco, a city whose pastel palette, sparkling bay, and landmark bridges are not the usual ingredients of the urban vista. But Brown also takes into account both the adjacent buildings and the design of the existing building. Which is to say, he looks both to the distant and immediate landscape for his design cues.

Such considerations paid off in this rooftop addition to a traditional residential three-story wood framed building. Brown continued the architectural agenda of the existing building—specifically the two-bay windows of the floor be-

low. The facade of the new penthouse is centered around single bay window that spans the two lower windows. But rounded glass greenhouse panels frame the bay window and throw a soft curve to the more linear plan of the existing facade. They also bring in additional natural daylight. Brown also specified that a trellis overhang these panels to provide shade. Painted the same soft beige as the rest of the building, the penthouse addition both continues the existing agenda and deviates from it in a subtle, elegant manner.

The interior of the addition, accommodating living, dining, and kitchen areas, follows an open plan. While its proportions maintain what Brown refers to as "the intimate scale and character of the existing building," the space is nevertheless spacious, open, airy. A deck adjacent to the kitchen offers sweeping views of the city skyline, the bay, and the Golden Gate Bridge. Thus the new construction is faithful to Brown's formula for

Left Bay view extension, exterior view

Above Bay view extension, interior view

rooftop building: "The top of the building should be a sky garden. It should be a special place for the inhabitants that is light, airy, and with outside spaces for lounging, eating and enjoying the views."

Photographs: Copyright, Christopher Irion

Left *Bay view extension, interior view*

Below Bay view extension, floor plans

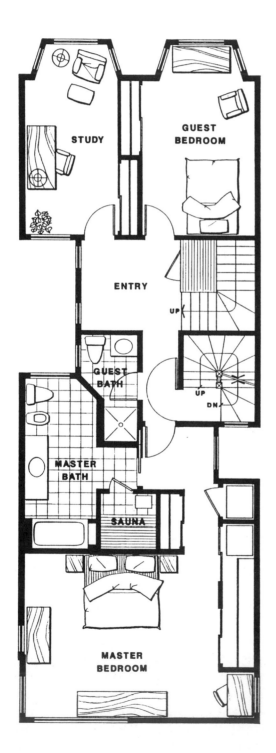

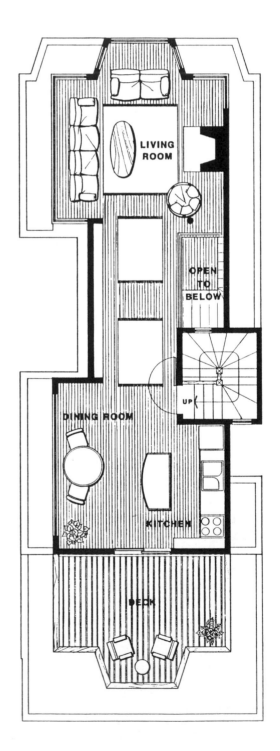

A Sky-Bound Air Stream
San Francisco, California

Theodore Brown & Partners, Inc.
San Francisco, California

Offering sweeping views of bay, bridge, and a panorama of the pastel colored city below, San Franscisco's Telegraph Hill may offer some of the most coveted pieces of real estate in the United States. The buildings of this neighborhood are constructed on a low, dense, residential scale, and the occasional rooftop addition may be the only practical means by which to expand this valuable urban space. Architect Theodore Brown has designed several such additions and observes that they may follow one of three basic formulas. First, the roof can serve as a vacant building lot on which a small house is constructed. Or, the existing structure can simply be extended in a design agenda that continues what has already been established below. Finally, the building can be layered; in such a case the top floor is not exactly a separate house but still varies in its design and character from the existing building.

Brown's addition to his own home, taking the form of a glass skyroom, is a variation on the third option. The existing building was a three-story wood-framed 1930s residential building. Brown's glazed sky room, measuring approximately twenty by twenty-six feet, is poised on top and accommodates dining and living areas, a kitchen and a small deck.

The interior is a study of cylindrical and rectilinear forms. The kitchen, mapped out by a circle of ceramic tile flooring, accommodates a rounded work area with range and sink. This area, with cabinetry that is also cylindrical, is juxtaposed to the rectilinear planes of the glass aerie itself. Finally, the satin-finish aluminum surfaces specified for the kitchen are a reflective counterpoint to the glass walls enclosing the sky room.

Left *Brown residence, uphill exterior view*

Above *Brown residence, exterior view*

Brown's rooftop addition is actually a duplex: Above the living area is a tiled rooftop and a silver, horseshoe-shaped pavilion. With its plaster facade painted silver and its rounded form, the construction seems to have aerodynamic origins; indeed, it may even suggest a sky-bound Air Stream trailer. Actually, the pavilion is a more practical appendage. Equipped with a dumbwaiter (also cylindrical), it is positioned directly above the kitchen and functions as a breakfast room. This uppermost region also continues the study of squares and cylinders. Railings are both curved and squared, as is the enigmatic form of the silver pavilion itself. Lighting has been installed between grout lines of the titled roof to illuminate the floor at night. Along with the curved railing, Brown observes, it evokes the sensibilities of a Japanese garden floating in the sky. (Achieving these subtle sensibilities required more pragmatic applications. A new foundation was poured at several locations to bear the weight of the new steel frames installed to support the garage doors below.)

"When you get to the top of the structure," explains Brown, "you find out if the architect is an artist and sculptor. Because how the building meets the sky is the domain of the artist/architect."

The observation is another variation on the premise that the rooftop, by nature, promotes a sense of invention, and Brown's Telegraph Hill addition proves the validity of the premise.

Photographs: Copyright, Christopher Irion

Below *Brown residence, floor plans*

Above Right *Brown residence, exterior view*

Below Right *View from terrace of Brown residence*

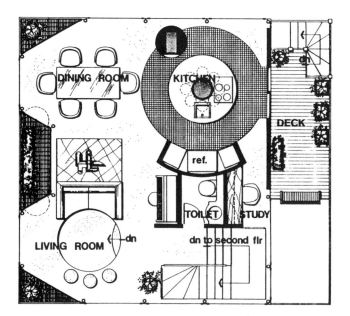

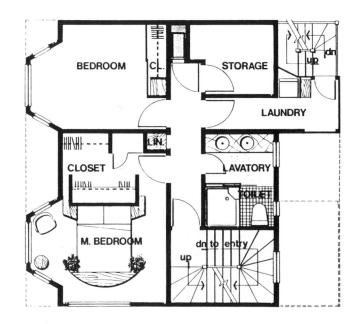

Skyline Solitude

New York, New York

P.M. Wheelwright Associates Architects
New York, New York

For one artist living in Manhattan, the rooftop of a six-story industrial loft building was the place to search out a private studio and retreat rather than an open area. As architect Peter Wheelwright explains it, "Less interested in a greenhouse exposure to the Manhattan skyline, the client wished for a more personal space with a sense of containment, place, and discretely framed views." With this in mind, the architect neverthless designed a studio—the client played classical guitar and was a painter—that was at once secluded and solitary as well as open and light-filled.

The inevitable sense of ascension established by the staircase leading to the rooftop is augmented by the tinted glass-block skylight positioned

directly overhead—itself an obvious means of bringing light and spaciousness into the small studio without compromising its privacy. The small, gabled sitting room at the top of the stairs serves as a receiving area and music room and is indeed a subdued, reclusive space. Wheelwright notes that, like "the apse of a church," it works to separate the studio from the space below.

The studio itself is boxlike, open and illuminated by a wall of south-facing windows. Here, sections of the tile floor have been cut away, drawing light to the interior of the sixth floor below. In the center of the studio stands a formal, built-in mahogany dias, which the architect notes monitors "the space and provides a focal point for contemplation and work." Curtains can be drawn across the southern wall of windows to assure privacy; they also suggest, especially during evening hours, that what lies on the skyscape beyond is sure theater.

Wheelwright has established a progression of

space from the staircase to the private receiving area, to the studio itself. "The terminus, such as it is," he says, "can be found in the work of the artist," which is surely the most appropriate conclusion in any working studio.

Photographs: Eliza Hicks

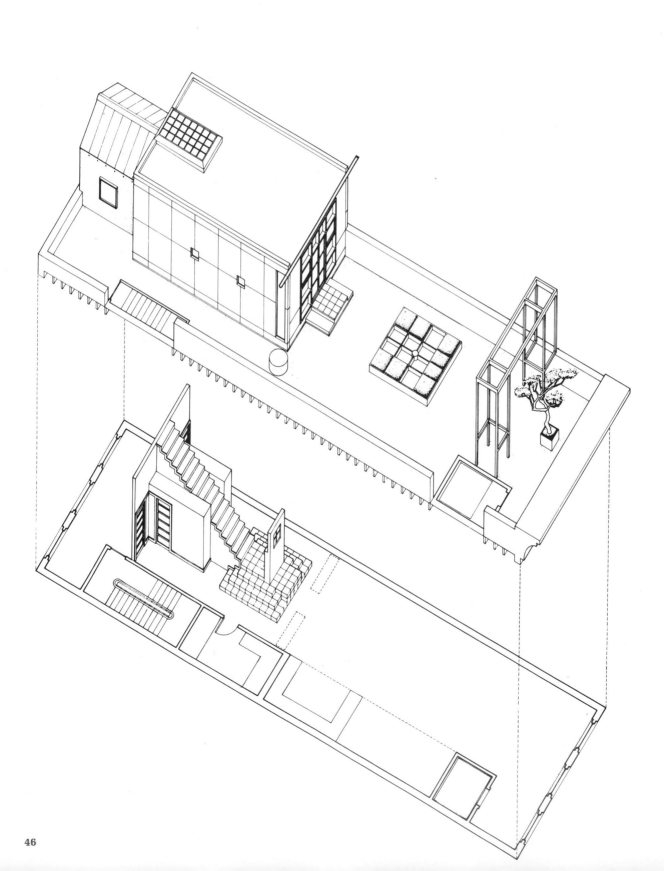

Compatibility out of Dissonance
New York, New York

P.M. Wheelwright
New York, New York

Architect Peter Wheelwright establishes the premise of this rooftop addition in unabashedly clinical terms: "Like a lot of New York City projects, this was a schizo structure." The addition referred to included a sun room with an expansive southern view alongside a more secluded, north-facing writing room, with solitary, framed views of the Chrysler Building to one side and the towers of the World Trade Center to the other. The space, then, was to be both public and private; dark and light; open and closed. But also like many other New York buildings, what may at first appear as schizophrenic discord later becomes a study in unique and unpredictable compatibility.

Because the roof itself was accessible to other

residents of the building, maintaining rooftop privacy was a part of the design strategy. The floor of the studio addition, then, is below the level of the deck. Such a layering of space causes the rooftop addition to be integral to both the apartment below (a master bedroom suite) and the roofline. Wheelwright observes that such layering also evokes the "scale and intimacy of a playhouse," a notion that is continued by a small ladder leading to a pitched deck, which itself becomes a small love seat at the very heart of the building.

The south-facing sun room, with its southern views, is equipped with a fireplace and built-in banquettes that suggest it as a social gathering place; exterior decking and a small fountain outdoors reinforce this impression. For the north-facing writing room, however, the architect has created a sense of solitude, not by physical distance but by a distinct separation: A slice of smoky mirrored glass installed between the

---

Left *Wheelwright rooftop writer's studio, exterior view*

Above *Deck of Wheelwright duplex rooftop*

rooftop house and its east wall suggests that this writing room may be a freestanding, separate zone, an apt metaphor, perhaps, for the imaginative travels that occur there.

The light sources for this writing room are all indirect. The purposes of these windows, states the architect, "has little to do with the sun or light. In fact, it's just the opposite. What they do instead is create a series of very private, discrete views." The east wall, then, has been punctured by small windows of colored glass which scatter jewellike patterns of light throughout the writing room during the day. Overhead is a small, round skylight. A slot of mirrored glass works as a frame for the distant towers of the World Trade Center to the south, while another window frames the Chrysler Building to the northeast.

Wheelwright has also used materials to define the varying functions of the rooftop. The mahogany and maple used for the desk in the writing room have been used for the banquette seating in the sun room. Flooring is honed black slate. Despite the two very different functions the small rooftop serves, there is a sense of synthesis rather than schism. In the end it may be the architect's invocation of Piet Mondrian that most eloquently states the design agenda: "Only the continual

and repeated union of opposites can bring about new progress; for new form arise from opposites dissolving into each other."

Photographs: Eliza Hicks

Photographs: (Right) Christopher Little

Below *Wheelwright studio, elevation drawing*

Above Right *Stairs leading to Wheelwright sun room and studio*

Below Right *Wheelwright rooftop writer's studio, interior view with sliver windows*

A Low-Rise, High-Tech Trailer
Venice, California

Morphosis
Santa Monica, California

The corrugated aluminum siding used for this rooftop renovation in Venice Beach reminded some neighbors of a trailer. It may not be a bad metaphor, although the path it follows is clearly vertical rather than horizontal. Instead of heading for the nearest roadside encampment, the construction points out a new stylistic direction in this modest neighborhood of more traditional beachside homes. Indeed, it stands out in the low-density residential community composed primarily of one- and two-story clapboard and stucco bungalows.

The original one-story, wood frame bungalow occupied a thirty-by-eighty foot lot with four-foot side yards and a fifteen-foot front setback. The lot was tight, with no room to build out. Architect Tom Mayne's predicament was how to enlarge the residence to accommodate a family with one

child. He did so by removing the building's original gable roof and building up, installing a second level with master bedroom and bath, and above that, a roof deck.

A column of space in the center of the new house accommodates the stairway that leads to these new areas. And a new expansive skylight—one that can be shaded—brings light into the master bedroom and living area alike. While Mayne has added only 300 square feet of living space (including the roof deck) to the existing 1200 square feet, illumination from the skylight makes the space seem greater.

The roof deck functions as an outdoor room. A low wall blocks out the wind while maintaining visual privacy from the active street life of Venice below. In the mild, southern California climate, such a "room" can be used throughout the year and adds significantly to the usable living space of the residence.

Sheathing the whole thing in corrugated alu-

Left and Above *Morphosis addition, exterior view*

minum was more than a high-tech trick. Available in two-by-ten foot lengths, the aluminum could be easily cut and installed to conform to the irregular contours of the house. Once it is sprayed with a polymer coating, the new siding also is maintenance-free, will not discolor, and can stand up to the severe stresses of the beach climate. A bright red painted metal railing outlines the profile of the new roofline. Venice has long been a community that has prided itself on being innovative, vaguely eccentric, and a short happy distance not only from Los Angeles, but from mainstream America as well. Indeed, if this rooftop addition evokes a trailer, it is one that travels that distance with ease.

Photographs: Dan Zimbaldi

Below *Morphosis addition, exterior view*

Below Right *Morphosis rooftop addition, exterior view*

Above Right *View into Morphosis outdoor room*

A Country Cabin
New York, New York

Karen L. Jacobson, Architect
New York, New York

Urban renovation has countless faces. Among those seen more frequently as urban real estate prices climb are those undertaken by a group of professionals who buy, divide, and renovate buildings in need of repair and then live in them. This was the case with this New York City, four-story brownstone. Built in the 1890s (for $20,000), it was first used as a residence, and later, during the Depression, became a rooming house. When the group of urban professionals, including architect Karen Jacobson, decided to purchase the row house in 1979, it had been carved into seventeen living units, all of them in a total shambles. Jacobson and her partners undertook the renovation themselves. And in the reorganization of the space, Jacobson was allotted a top floor studio apartment—and roof rights.

Left   *View from across the street of Jacobson cabin*

Above   *Jacobson cabin, bedroom*

"I wanted to play up the feeling of a cottage," explains Jacobson of the subsequent rooftop addition she designed. And the casement shutter windows and pitched roof do exactly that. While the other buildings adjacent to hers on the block are similar brownstones, behind them is a row of much taller apartment buildings that loom, Jacobson notes, "like a ridge of mountains," further suggesting the geography of a more rural hillside.

But what is especially ingenious about the addition, which houses a small hallway (measuring eight feet by eight feet) and bedroom (measuring twelve feet by twelve feet), is that despite its seemingly rural format, the structure is not as anti-urban as it may first seem: Its triangular forms also refer to the brownstone's pediment and to the form of its existing triangular skylights.

Jacobson confronted two major construction problems that often come with rooftop territory: The roof joists were not designed to support the same weight as the floors below; and the roof had, approximately, a six-foot pitch. Jacobson's solution was to build a new platform on the roof that would be supported by two steel beams running from parapet to parapet. Each weighed between six and seven hundred pounds and were hoisted from street level by crane.

Built three feet from the rear edge of the brownstone, the cabin, a structure of concrete blocks, metal studs, and stucco, avoids any direct view of the city below; for this reason it seems more remote from the urban grid than a mere four floors. "It seems to exist on a whole separate plane," notes Jacobson, for whom privacy was a cherished commodity. All the same, future plans include a wood deck in front of the cottage; the deck will benefit from ample sunlight and further evoke the sense of being a country retreat.

Photographs: Dan Cornish

Below *Jacobson cabin, exterior view*

Above Right *Jacobson cabin, bath*

Below Right *Jacobson cabin, bedroom*

A Neoclassical Cottage
Tokyo, Japan

Robert A.M. Stern Architects
New York, New York

The five-story office building in downtown Tokyo was already under construction when Robert A. M. Stern Architects became associated with the project. "The original facade," says project architect Grant Marani, "was nondescript, a little banal, with strip windows and stone panels, alternating bands of stone and glass. We tried to install a little elegance and grace."

Although the basic form of the building had been established, the new facade as well as the plans for the two-story, residential penthouse do exactly that. The architects explain that the facade was designed "as a response to the abstracted somber classicism of the British Embassy (its immediate neighbor) and the client's preference for traditional western architecture." The resulting

facade has a black granite base and pilasters with green granite inserts; it is a study of gradations of black, from the deep black at the base to the black stucco body of the building which terminates with the warmer charcoal stucco of the penthouse facade.

The building is all the more noticeable in a neighborhood where most of the other buildings have been constructed in white brick, tile, or pale masonry. Indeed, as Marani explains, the classicism of the British Embassy—somewhat staid, but with an individual style and grace nevertheless—with its overtones of British colonial architecture, was the only design cue in the immediate urban landscape.

As the architects admit, the building works as a podium, a solid and elegant building base for the penthouse, the neoclassical cottage on its roof. The design of the penthouse, known as the Bancho House and measuring close to four thousand square feet, correlates with that of the building

---

Above *Bancho House, perspective drawing*

Left *Bancho House, exterior view*

below. This is not an eccentric marriage of styles but rather an integrated whole; building and penthouse read as a single building. The setback of the penthouse allows for a grand terrace garden which itself looks over the treetops of the formal British Embassy garden immediately below and the gardens of the Imperial Palace beyond. Densely planted pergolas at either end of the terrace work both to maintain privacy and to emphasize the southeast view of the city.

The architecture of Tokyo is typical contemporary urban eclectic; minimal, monochromatic, and modern on the one hand; chaotic, visually tumultuous, and loud on the other. The installation here of more somber British classicism both adds to the eclectic landscape and is a stylistic respite from it.

Drawings: Courtesy of Robert A. M. Stern Architects

Photographs: © Peter Aaron/ESTO

Below   *Bancho House, floor plans*

Right   *Bancho House, elevation drawings*

ROOF PLAN

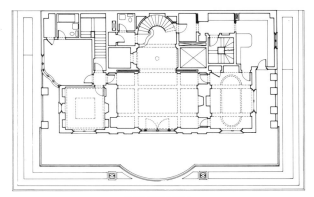

SIXTH FLOOR PLAN

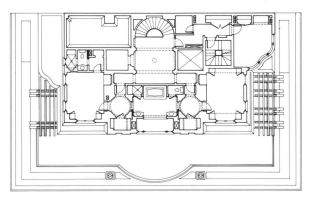

SEVENTH FLOOR PLAN

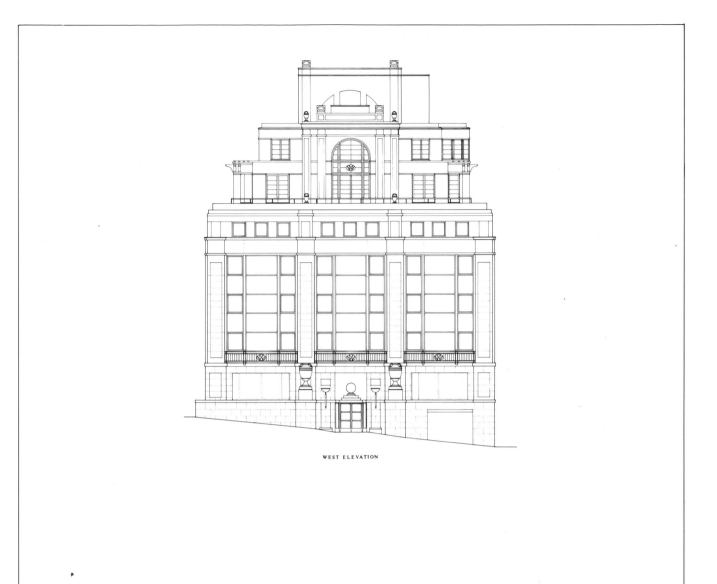

WEST ELEVATION

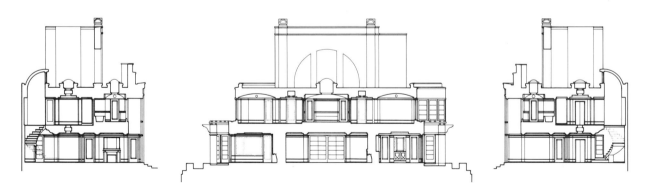

RUSTIC RETREATS:

Country Houses, Gazebos, Gardens, Pools, and Tool Sheds on Urban Rooftops

Introduction

Pluralism is the keynote of contemporary urban architecture. A single city block may be an exhibit of beaux arts, international, Georgian, Edwardian, and Victorian styles, to mention only a few. While some cities may persist in encouraging a single building style, such stylistic consistency is gradually being replaced by architectural diversity. The rooftop, of course, is the zone that most encourages this inventiveness. With fewer aesthetic or stylistic restrictions than those that generally govern earthbound buildings, the design of rooftop constructions has a broader range. It should come as no surprise, then, to find on the rooftop not only the variety of urban dwellings we have shown so far, but a broad representation of country houses and gardens as well.

To be sure, the often hostile and aggressive pace of urban life has given country living a nostalgic appeal. The geographic privacy and the intimacy with the natural environment, the sense of distance and quietude are all qualities integral to rural life. These are qualities that are often equally desirable and out of reach for the urban dweller. And while these qualities may be utterly absent in the modern urban environment, the distance, cost, and frustration of commuting to a country house may put them even further out of reach. But, if they are to be negotiated, the place such negotiations occur may be on the roof.

For the urban gardener, what better plot is available? If space and light are the necessary ingredients for the garden, then the rooftop may be the only place to find them, and the often lush and extravagant gardens that can be encountered on blacktop exist in blissful incongruity with their gritty environment. Urban gardens, and how organic matter as such can transform the rooftop into a peaceable, albeit small, kingdom are a subject unto themselves.

Another matter altogether are those optimists and extremists who install not simply gardens on the roof, but the entire country house itself. Not content with tending carefully potted plants or the occasional raised beds of vegetables, they persist in constructing garden houses, gazebos, and other structures one would be more likely to find in a rural pasture or woodland than on a city roof. Whether it is a bedroom suite, study, or guesthouse, these rooftop additions function not simply as extra space, but as extra space that is defined by a rural rather than urban context. Sited within a rooftop garden, these particular rooftop additions are designed not simply to increase the usable space of the existing house or apartment, but to provide a link with the outdoors—not the urban outdoors, but a more organic, vegetative environment.

Landscape architect Daniel Stewart likens the rooftop climate and environment to the seashore, with its fierce winds and severe weather conditions. No matter. There is sunshine, space, and solitude as well, and the stylistic restrictions of these macroenvironments are only those posed by imagination or budget.

That it is an outdoors that is manufactured and contrived in no way lessens its appeal. Indeed, these rooftop country houses are altogether illusory. The trellis covered with climbing plants or perhaps a row of evergreens may indeed have been installed to obscure the unsightly masonry walls of a neighboring building; still, it is this very component of fantasy that gives these abbreviated rural landscapes their charm and appeal. A cottage sited in a bucolic rural habitat of some rose bushes and wisteria, is an irresistible proposition for a culture that proposes to have it all.

Overleaf *Exterior view of facade and garden of Kelso residence*

Left *Halasz roof garden, exterior view*

Brownstone Botanics
New York, New York

Kelso Architects
Kailua, Hawaii

The four-story brownstone in New York City had been divided into a series of apartments when architects Michael and Lisa Kelso purchased the upper two floors. In combining a studio apartment on the third floor with a third- and fourth-floor duplex, and restructuring the third and fourth floor roofs, they intended not simply to increase the usable living space of the co-op, but to create a country house—a tall order for Manhattan's congested Upper West Side.

The Kelsos achieved their hopes through a number of devices, but primarily and most dramatically by replacing the fourth floor shed with a penthouse master bedroom suite. They also replaced the tar and gravel rooftop, approximately fifteen by thirty-five feet, with decking in remov-

able sections, fences, planters, and handrails, and an abundance of greenery and flowers. Indeed, as Lisa Kelso observes of the subsequent brownstone botanics, "The intimate, residential style of the master bedroom facade reflects a country house. There is a profusion of plants, roses outside the master bath window, a trellis with wisteria, lilac bushes, sweet pea vines, even a maple tree to help attain a country feeling."

More than flora, however, suggests this is a rural habitat. The facade of the new penthouse, approximately fifteen by twenty-one feet, has been sheathed in white clapboard, and the two windows overlooking the garden are wood and single glazed. The peaked roof over the entrance also evokes a familiar residential scale. Metal security bars, which may not be common on the windows of most other country houses, have been painted and aligned with the window mullions "to avoid the prison effect," as Lisa Kelso notes. Materials used in the interior include tradition-

---

Above *View from master bedroom suite of Kelso residence*

Left *Kelso residence, exterior*

al hardwood floors, wood moldings, and painted gypsum board walls. Indeed, scale, materials, and the lush garden all suggest that this is a country cottage, a notion that may even be perpetuated by the very contrast it creates with the massive masonry apartment building looming behind it.

The architects also installed a rear exterior stairway connecting the third floor kitchen and living areas to the upper roof deck. The section of the third floor roof beneath this stairway measures about eight by thirteen feet. In its new function as an herb garden and potting shed, it is perhaps the greatest anomaly of all in this urban makeover.

As in other rooftop renovations, the architects also wanted to bring natural daylight to the third floor dining and living areas below. They did so by installing a metal skylight, also sheathed in white clapboard. With its glazed pyramid profile, the skylight at once makes for its own miniature garden folly and echoes the other eccentric forms of the city roofscape, from the pointed roofline of a nearby water tower to the more exotic peaks and turrets of distant skyscrapers.

Photographs: Elliott Kaufman

Above Right *Kelso residence, interior*

Below Right *Floor plan of Kelso roof garden and master suite*

Below *Kelso residence, section drawing.*

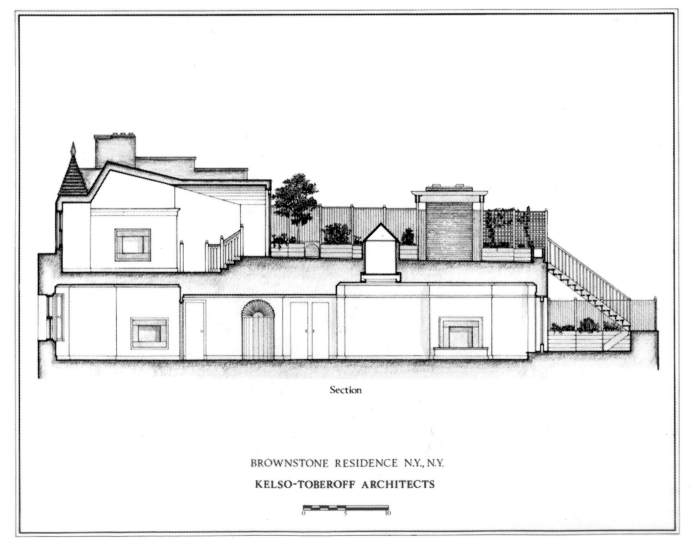

Section

BROWNSTONE RESIDENCE N.Y., N.Y.

KELSO-TOBEROFF ARCHITECTS

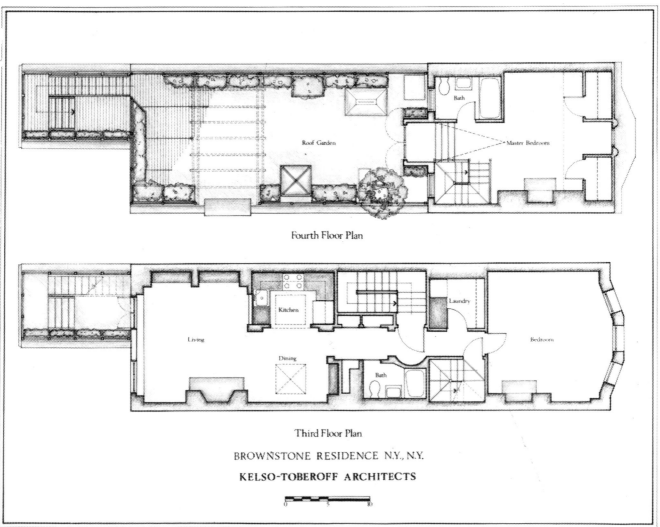

Fourth Floor Plan

Third Floor Plan

BROWNSTONE RESIDENCE N.Y., N.Y.

KELSO-TOBEROFF ARCHITECTS

Peaceful Pavilions
New York, New York

**Wurmfeld Associates, P.C.
and Stewart & Kleinman, Landscape Architects**

The rooftop of the seventeen-story prewar apartment building in New York City had already been paved with quarry tiles and lined with planters when the previous tenants of this penthouse converted the rooftop to an urban terrace. Architect Michael Wurmfeld's clients, a family with children, had a more demanding agenda. Rather than simply using the rooftop as a garden, they wanted to transform it to a lush, sheltered courtyard, an urban oasis and private space for family use and entertaining. It was also to accommodate a child's playhouse and a private office.

The architects organized the space both by dense layering of plant life and by built constructions. Instead of simply adding on to the existing penthouse, the architects designed a series of

separate structures, what Wurmfeld calls "a grouping of pavilions." Indeed, the placement of the structures constitutes a deliberate composition. Positioned at diagonal ends of the terrace, the two small buildings "reorient the gridded internal space and control views across the garden and to the surrounding urban context." The pavilions themselves have been designed as a cube and half cube in a plan that emphasizes the small grid of the garden in the larger grid of the urban environment.

The pavilions capitalize on the abundant natural light that illuminates rooftop acreage. For the north-facing walls, the architects specified a transparent Plexiglas surface. For walls with a southern exposure, they installed instead a translucent fiberglass shoji-screen paneling that allowed light to permeate the interior without bringing excessive heat. The same material is used for the roof of the studio. As both structures have electric heating as well as air-conditioning,

---

Left *Overview of Wurmfeld garden and pavilion*

Above *Wurmfeld rooftop, greenhouse studio.*

the insulating properties of the fiberglass panels make them all the more practical a surfacing material.

The architects also installed stainless steel wire trellises to both define the different outdoor areas and frame particular views. The presence of the trellises, along with the crisp grid of the two buildings, almost evokes an industrial aesthetic. It is an aesthetic that is juxtaposed, of course, with the softer and denser layering of plant life—rhododendrun bushes, azaleas, and even dogwood trees and a row of pines. "In time," observes Wurmfeld, "plant materials covering the trellises will soften their machinelike quality."

Landscape architect Daniel Stewart observes that what is unique about this rooftop agenda is that it is a sheltered, intimate environment. Unlike so many rooftops that are open to expansive views, this is more private, with an inward orientation. "The analogy I like to use for the landscaping of most terraces," he explains, "is that of the seashore. Terraces tend to be windy and exposed to severe weather conditions. Japanese black pine, rough, tough grasses, and rose bushes do well there. But on this rooftop we were able to use plants that need more sheltered areas." Indeed, along with the fencing around the entire terrace, plants have been used to structure the rooftop; to enhance some views, and to hide others; an unsightly brick wall adjacent to the greenhouse studio, for example, is concealed by a row of pines. Together with the rooftop pavilions, the plants create a series of intimate, enclosed "rooms," private sanctuaries amidst urban cacophony.

Below *Wurmfeld roof garden, axonometric drawing*

Right *Wurmfeld roof garden, playhouse and studio views*

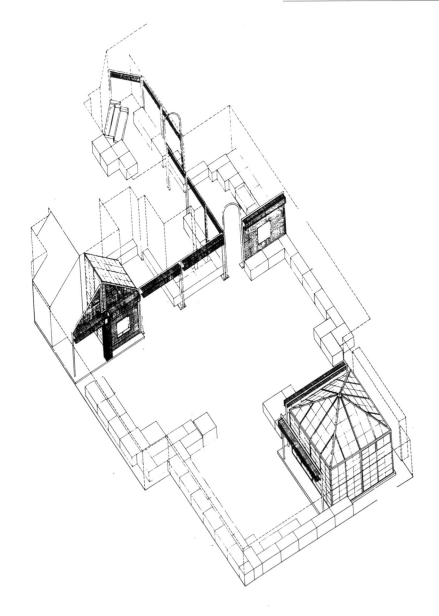

High-Rise Horticulture
Boston, Massachusetts

Imre Halasz
Boston, Massachusetts

"The garden was conceived as an alternative to a country home, a place where family and guests might enjoy sunshine and flowers by commuting up a flight of stairs," explains architect Imre Halasz of his own rooftop addition. Indeed, as Halasz and Sylvia Sutton did not own a car when they planned and built their rooftop addition, such a brief commute was all the more practical. Constructed on the roof of a nine-story apartment building in Boston's Back Bay, the light-filled aerie works both as a private study and as the access to what the architect refers to as "the high-rise horticulture" of the garden. The garden itself works as a series of open-air rooms with expansive views across the Back Bay to Cambridge, and east to Beacon Hill and downtown Boston.

The crisp, pointed roofline of the penthouse adds to the already eclectic roofline of the immediate urban landscape. From one angle, the penthouse can be viewed against the soaring glass facade of the John Hancock Tower. Seen from another view, its most immediate neighbor is the more ornate appendage of the First Baptist Church—the Tower of the Holy Beanblowers where carved figures in flowing garments blow their trumpets over the less celestial throngs below.

The penthouse itself is not without its own celestial aspirations. Indeed, the angle of the roofline is a trajectory that suggests, if not immediate flight, a sense of sudden ascension. A wood frame and glass structure measuring about eight by twenty feet, the penthouse functions as a study for Sutton, who is a writer. (As a concession to the notion of a garden pavilion, the study was also equipped with a refrigerator for the cool drinks that garden labor inevitably demands.)

Above *Halasz residence, exterior view*

Left *Halasz roof garden, exterior view*

The living area below is connected to the penthouse by an open staircase. Already an expansive, flowing space that accommodates living, dining, and den areas, it virtually soars since the installation of the stairway leading upward in a line that visually anticipates the steep roofline of the penthouse. Sutton explains that the penthouse structure was constructed before breaking through the roof. The staircase was built afterwards. Fortunately, construction occurred while the entire building was being converted to condominiums, so that the effect of the additional, often traumatic rooftop construction was minimized.

The gardens themselves have been planned as a series of very different rooms. Four-foot-by-four-foot removable sections of redwood decking were positioned over the tar-and-gravel surface, and wooden fences were installed to enclose a perennial garden, support climbing plants, and act as windscreens. "The east side of the garden," explains Halasz "is a quiet, shady, private place for thinking, reading and dozing. The plantings there consist of hardy trees and climbers plus low-maintenance, modestly blooming perennials. By contrast, the sunnier, more spacious west side is

the living-dining area, planted principally with colorful annuals and two dozen rose bushes." Including roses, an evergreen border, geraniums, hibiscus, marigolds, and numerous climbers, the lush garden is more redolent of a rural landscape. Indeed, Sutton recalls being startled by the incongruous and decidedly nonurban relationship that she developed with her immediate rooftop neighbors, also urban gardeners, as they traded seeds and plantings against the backdrop of the urban skyline.

Photographs: Imre Halasz

Below Right *Halasz rooftop addition, interior view*

Below Left *Open stairway leading to Halasz rooftop*

Right Top and Bottom *Arborvitae of Halasz rooftop*

A Floating Pool

New York, New York

Walter F. Chatham, Architect
New York, New York

Architect Walter Chatham and his wife had already renovated the light-filled top floor of this twelve-story, steel frame loft building in Manhattan's Soho before the rooftop could become part of their plans. The penthouse, however, became available when the Chathams' second child was expected, and the Chathams decided to give the children and their nanny their own rooftop apartment, with three bedrooms, a kitchen, and a dining/living room area. The rooftop itself, once standard-issue blacktop, became a communal space, serving as both a playground for the children and a serene retreat for adults.

If translucent and transparent materials are naturals for the abundant light flooding rooftop building plots, Chatham doubled the possible effects by using glass and water. A wall of glass blocks that fills the penthouse with natural light during daylight hours and a small shimmering Japanese pool together work to separate the deck and rooftop garden from the penthouse apartment. Indeed, the surface of glass and the surface of water create a glistening dialogue of light. By day, natural light diffused through the wall of glass bricks throws flickering patterns of light across the walls and floor of the children's dining area. At night, it is the interior lighting from the penthouse that shimmers outdoors in the small, reflecting pool.

The pool is deceptively shallow; only six inches deep, it is actually a plywood box lined with fiberglass and scattered with black Japanese pebbles that give it a luminous depth and darkness. But for all its aesthetic charm, the pool serves a practical purpose. "I actually developed it as a hydroengineering project," confesses Chatham. The pool works as a retention pool for

---

the angles roof's drainage system. All the same, with its dark surface and concrete stepping stones, the holding tank is indeed a more mysterious, floating pool and is reminiscent of more bucolic environs.

The deck has been constructed in pressure-treated fir, in three tiers, in a raised progression that draws the eye to the urban vista beyond, making it all the more dramatic. The pointed roof of the small, corrugated aluminum tool shed is its own condensed folly. While the material nods in acknowledgement to warehouse vernacular, the form mimics the grander profiles of the not-so-distant Manhattan skyline.

Below   *Chatham rooftop, "reading room"*

Right   *Chatham rooftop, tool shed*

ROOFTOP FOLLIES:
The Architecture of Provocation

Introduction

In his introduction to George Mott's book *Follies and Pleasure Pavilions,* Gervase Jackson-Stops asks:

> What is it that gives these buildings their particular excitement? Why does the pulse quicken as a distant tower comes into view at the end of an avenue or a winding woodland path suddenly breaks into a clearing to reveal a pyramid, a grotto, or a long-forgotten bath house. Surprise has always been central to the idea of the folly: What you find may be Classical or Gothic, Chinese or Egyptian; made of tree roots or tufa, shells or bones; a monument to a wife or a horse; a place for keeping tigers or chickens. Legends cluster around such buildings. . . If there is a common link among them it is, in fact, the element of fantasy, for wheras the design of the country house had to conform to a conventional lifestyle, and cope with the practicalities of everyday existence, the plans for a garden building could afford to be more experimental and imaginative. (George Mott, *Follies and Pleasure Pavilions,* New York, Harry N. Abrams, 1989, p. 8)

While rooftop additions must address the practicalities of everyday living, there is a certain category of such additions that is defined by similar elements of the fantastic. Although these rooftop follies are each unique, they are nonetheless linked together by the astonishment they evoke in their viewers (if not inhabitants). These are dreamlike extravaganzas that one does not expect to confront in the gritty reality of the urban landscape.

It is one thing to be astonished in the pastoral landscape of England; for all its tranquil beauty, it is a landscape of the predictable—which perhaps is exactly why it invites the intrigue and exoticism of architectural follies so persuasively. The juxtaposition of the serene natural landscape with more startling and capricious manmade constructions may be irresistible. Astonishment in the urban landscape is another matter altogether. By its very nature, the cityscape is unpredictable; we are accosted at all sides by the unexpected— in behavior, in events, and in architecture. To construct a folly—a habitat designed to astonish— then, is a tall order; it is a tricky proposition to construct a building that is meant to provoke when a constant state of provocation is a pre-existing condition of the landscape. Yet it is exactly this sense of aesthetic provocation and astonishment that typifies the rooftop folly.

Like their rural predecessors in the gardens of Great Britain, some of these more contemporary urban follies are designed as retreats, as places for solitary meditation and reflection. That a place for such quietude can be constructed in the midst of urban cacophony can itself seem fantastic. A garage roof in Tokyo is not the customary locale for a traditional Shinto shrine, and that architect Atsushi Kitagawara has placed such a shrine there only intensifies its aura of mystery and tranquility. Indeed, there is an element of reversal here. Whereas English garden follies were provocative constructions in a quiet landscape, some urban follies may be defined by the degree of serenity they provide in a more riotous environment.

But there is more to it than this. If the rooftop is the landscape of invention, these follies embody this truth to its fullest. And while they certainly address the practical demands of everyday life, they also exploit outrageously the stylistic freedom that the rooftop represents. The rooftop law office designed by Coop Himmelblau is not only visually unrelated to the building below; it is disconnected from anything earthbound at all, ideological or aesthetic. It is a marvel of deviation. On the other hand, there is the Petal House whose unfolding roofline originates in conventional roof forms; it then quietly explodes these forms and freezes that explosion in midair—an instance of the astonishing emerging from the mundane. Finally, there are the inevitable cases where the building itself is a folly, where the building base itself explores exotic architectural forms and the rooftop is the cap or conclusion to this search.

Rooftop follies have been inspired by images from Dali to Disney. And indeed, they bring a sense of excitement and intrigue to the urban landscape. But apart from that, they remind us that architecture can be provocative, experimental, and functional, not necessarily in that order. In traditional garden follies, practicality was secondary to whimsy. Here, on the roof, although it sometimes seems that the practical functions the follies serve are almost incidental, pragmatism and whimsy go hand in hand.

Overleaf *Gehry's rooftop village, exterior view*

Left *The Petal House, exterior view*

A Rooftop Visitation
Vienna, Austria

Coop Himmelblau
Los Angeles, California
and
Vienna, Austria

It was, among other things, a rare conjunction of architecture and language that occurred on this street corner in Vienna. Or perhaps it could be described as a collision, though one graceful and precise. The architects' studio is called Coop Himmelblau, German for "Blue Sky Cooperative." And the law firm that was their client is situated on the corner of Falkestrasse, or "Falcon Street." Say the architects, "We did not, in this case, think of a bird or wings, although it was hard not to do so." Indeed, the rooftop addition that was created here brings to mind the arrested flight of some exotic urban bird. Unlike the standard-issue pigeons found nesting on sills and drainpipes, this hybrid of glass and steel wings has crash-

landed on the rooftop in an altogether more dramatic and startling manner.

The two-story addition is the expansion of a law office situated on the first and second floors of the existing building. The rooftop addition includes a meeting room, three office units, a reception area, and adjacent rooms. "While making the design," explain the architects, "we envisioned a reversed lightning bolt and a taut arc." And in its form and energy alike, this addition supports the notion of a visitation from some unfamiliar stratosphere. A steel backbone and trusses are spanned by sheets of curved glazing, while one section of the roofline has been constructed as a series of folds. But there is the question, then, of whether these folds are closing in repose or expanding for flight. There is an interior balcony and an outdoor terrace. Illumination comes in spots, streaks, and wider washes of light, somewhat the way it appears on the skyline itself. Startling juxtapositions of open, glazed surfaces

---

Above *Coop Himmelblau law office addition, exterior view*

Left *Exterior view across the terrace to the interior balcony of Coop Himmelblau addition.*

---

and folded, linear surfaces control the light, creating vistas or blocking them altogether.

"There are no alcoves or turrets on the roof," say the architects. "No context of proportions, materials, or color, but instead, a visualized line of energy which, coming from the street, spans the project, thus breaking the existing roof and thereby opening it." To reflect the position of this addition on the urban skyscape, the architects have taken as their design cue not the more restrained forms and ornament of the existing building or urban grid, but the imagery of the sky itself, a province of the grand, the unknown, and the unexpected. The imagery includes sheets of light, a folded wing, a bolt of lightening. Although the rooftop itself is only about seventy feet above the ground, the height of its invention and of the aesthetic risks it takes are much higher.

Photographs: Gerald Zugmann

Below *View of Coop Himmelblau conference room, with the interior balcony to the right*

Right *Coop Himmelblau addition, view of conference room under the folded roof*

Freeway Flower
Los Angeles, California

Eric Owen Moss, Architect
Culver City, California

The freeways of Los Angeles carry not simply the city's commerce, but a heavy symbolic load as well. And when one considers the numbers of hours the city's residents log in there, the vernacular roadside architecture of the city isn't what it could or should be. Eric Moss's Petal House, so named for the unfolding leaves of its roofline that bloom precariously and unexpectedly on the edge of the Santa Monica Freeway, is an exception to the rule. Taking a standard-issue, two-story, 1100 square-foot, wood frame tract house, Moss has negotiated a roadside attraction that is meant to be seen as much as it is a place from which to do the seeing.

The renovation and expansion of the house included a new master suite and bath, a new

kitchen, an expanded living room, and a new studio and guest quarters. Moss retained elements of the existing building, explaining that "a careful effort was made to understand and extend the essential qualities of both the existing house and the immediate neighborhood, in particular the roof forms, the area's dominant formal feature. Typical shed roof forms are reiterated in the kitchen, living room/porch, and guest extensions." In the kitchen, for example, the eaves of the original shed roof of the house provide cover for the oven and refrigerator.

But it is the folly at the roofline that blows out not simply the roof itself but these conventional forms of the conventional tract house/bungalow used below. This is a folly that is not a stylistic departure from the building below, but a stylistic explosion of it; and it is not so much a rooftop construction as it is a manipulation of the very roof form itself. The four leaves, or "petals" of the pyramid-shaped roof have been folded back at

Left and Above *Petal House, exterior views*

93

varying angles above the second floor master suite. These leaves, then, work as partial walls, creating a semiprivate outdoor room and sun deck, as well as a sculptural profile on the flatlands of the West Los Angeles landscape. The views from this rooftop—of Westwood, Century City, and, of course, the freeway itself—appear in slices, at the corners where the leaves have been folded back from one another.

The varying angles of the "leaves" have been determined by function as well as aesthetics. The slope of the southern wall permits the sun to warm the hot tub area and deck and is supported by the plywood frame that the hot tub has been built into; the northern "fin" is supported by a bench and the eastern fin by wing walls for the exterior access ladder; and the western fin is supported by a large box for the hot tub equipment. A web of one-inch nylon ropes connects—visually, if not structurally—the different leaves. That these leaves have been so delicately laced together also reinforces, indeed exploits, the sense of subtle peril that the precarious rooftop site invariably brings with it.

Photographs: © Tim Street-Porter/ESTO

Rooftop Village
Santa Monica, California

Frank O. Gehry & Associates, Inc.
Santa Monica, California

Many rooftop additions tend to be discreet constructions that observe a sense of decorum regarding setback regulations. While the rooftop locale may afford its residents solitude, many such additions defer politely nonetheless to the established style of the other buildings in the immediate neighborhood, zoning regulations, and the sensibilities of the neighbors. Situated so that they may be only partially visible from the street, rooftop additions may come into view suddenly and unexpectedly, their element of astonishment a result not only of their eccentric form but of their secluded location as well. Quite the opposite is true of this residence in Santa Monica designed by Frank Gehry.

Conceived not so much as a penthouse but as an entire small village, the addition tumbles over and around an existing four-story pink stucco apartment building. There is a glazed facade and a pale blue dome, a corrugated tin shed, more of the pink stucco, a box of black granite, and finally a ziggurat coated with gold auto-body paint. Gehry's architecture has always been distinguished by juxtapositions of inexpensive and more costly lavish building materials, but juxtapositions of expense are the least of what he has created here. Clearly, this is the architecture of fantasy, an affluence of imagery that is almost overload, a familiar commodity that Los Angeles has built its reputation on.

In his survey of British garden follies, George Mott observes that "a nodding acquaintance with the classical world was an obligatory attribute of the eighteenth-century gentleman, and the manifestation of this familiarity might be a piece of antiquity in one's own backyard—temples, ruined aqueducts, and miniature pantheons all

_____

Above *Gehry's rooftop village, exterior view*

Left *Gehry rooftop addition, exterior view*

found their way into the gardens of those who could afford them." Gehry has more than a nodding acquaintance with architectural history, and the resulting pluralism that shows up in his work—the pile-up of architectural imagery—parodies the more restrained display found in English gardens.

But Gehry's work is not a question of visual cacophony. Gehry has built his reputation on layering seemingly incongruous slices of form, material, color, texture, indeed whole segments of architectural history to construct an astonishingly sensible and logical whole. The fourth floor of the building in Santa Monica was demolished, and in its place this series of objects installed. But as dissimilar as these added forms are on the exterior, the interior of the duplex—the studio, bedrooms, living/dining area, kitchen, staircases, and baths—has been assembled as a logical, continuous whole. Ample glazing washes the interior with natural light, allowing the different spaces to flow into one another and offering a sweeping view of the towers of Century City and Los Angeles.

Says Gehry in a statement about the house, "The dome over the kitchen comes from Israel or that part of the world, and the curved stairway comes from many of the pictures that were shown to me of curved stairways. The use of marble and special tile was strong client input. I invited the client to do some of the decor and participate in some of those considerations, so that when the building was finished it would be a collaboration." Frank Gehry, (*The Architecture of Frank Gehry*, New York, New York, Rizzoli International Publications, Inc., 1986, p 181)

Indeed, Gehry's client was an artist with her own clearly established aesthetics, clearly established in that it embraced its own diversity. Not surprisingly, then, the same stylistic mosaic distinguishes the collaborative interior. Memphis and art deco cowhide furniture are thrown together. There are collections of antique dolls and antique teapots. Surfaces of brilliantly glazed ceramic tiles, etched glass, blue tinted mirrors, and corrugated metal columns create their own dissonant rhythms. All of these might easily be the ingredients of aesthetic anarchy. That the diversity is not jarring but rather is reassuring, exuberant, and cohesive is testimony to the architect's clear, single vision.

Photographs: Michael Moran

Above *Early sketches for Frank Gehry's rooftop images*

Above Right *Gehry rooftop village, section drawing and floor plans*

Below Right *Gehry rooftop, interior view*

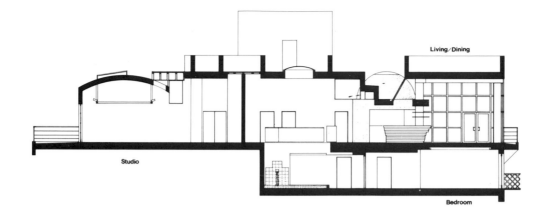

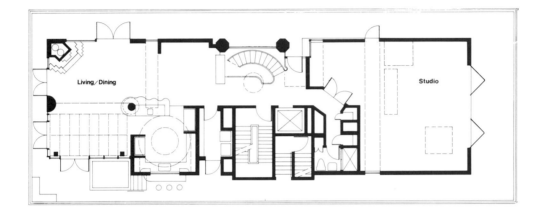

A Rooftop Teahouse
Tokyo, Japan

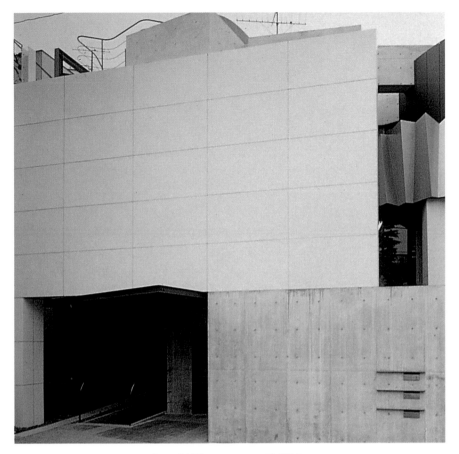

Atsushi Kitagawara + ILCD inc.
Tokyo, Japan

If the rooftop is the place where urban dwellers may most peaceably find solitude, architect Atsushi Kitagawara has given this search new rewards. The building he has designed in Tokyo to accommodate both his own studio and an apartment for an elderly widow (who is a tea master) has tatami rooms and a small tea house tucked into its low rooftop. That these traditional chambers of quiet ritual should coexist with the more jarring urban environment was part of the architect's agenda of provocative juxtapositions.

A pleated sheet of galvanized steel, almost golden in color, shields the sliver of rooftop garden from the street. To one side is an almost threatening black wedge; to the other a more placid, pale grid. This combination of volumes might be a study of incongruity, but strangely, they seem to reside in tranquil coexistence here.

Whereas the exterior is composed of a series of abstract forms, the interior is more straightforward. Natural materials have been used inside the chambers of the pavilion and natural light filters through traditional shoji screens. With polished woods, stones, and a bed of black pebbles, the interior evokes a more rural outdoors.

The tea ceremony itself represents a retreat from the clamor of daily life. And the traditional architecture of the teahouse maps out a harmony with the natural world. Patterns of light and shadow may be the only ornamentation. By inserting this teahouse on a modern city rooftop, Kitagawara is perhaps recognizing that this world of the spirit can reside within the more chaotic context of the modern city; and if the city is a place of relentless contradictions, its architecture can both represent these differences and bring them to a reconciliation.

Photographs: Paul Warchol

Above *Kitagawara rooftop teahouse, exterior view*

Right *Kitagawara rooftop teahouse, interior view*

A Shinto Shrine
Tokyo, Japan

Atsushi Kitagawara + ILCD inc.
Tokyo, Japan

Atsushi Kitagawara's work is indeed the architecture of provocation, and the architect himself has labeled this project "the architecture of irony." Certainly, the placement of a small Shinto shrine atop a garage creates a contrast not simply of building styles but of function and spirit as well. Contextualism, the architect seems to be saying, has no place in the modern city where things change at a dizzying pace. An unpredictable future is not simply a consideration of his work, but its very premise.

Contradictions abound in Miaonkaku, the office building and shrine the architect designed in Tokyo. The temple's traditional architectural detailing, craftsmanship, brilliant hues, and patterning are all the more startling and evocative when placed alongside the masonry and glass of its more modern neighbors. Positioned on a small concrete garage and beneath the shimmering glass facade of an office building, the shrine perhaps says something of those unexpected districts in which the world of the spirit may emerge. And while one hardly likes to reduce the architect's work to such overt symbols, Kitagawara seems to be saying something by so neatly sandwiching accommodations for the soul between accommodations for the automobile and for corporate commerce. Through all his choices, Kitagawara interprets the modern city—a place where materials, styles, functions, and indeed spirits collide. His buildings exploit these collisions, making the most of the drama and their grace.

There is also the reversal of the rooftop folly being such a traditional structure. Most rooftop building design is, by its very nature, an abbreviated flight of fantasy that uses a more convention-

---

Above *Rooftop Shinto shrine, side view*

Left *Rooftop Shinto shrine, exterior view*

al building form below as both a building base and a base of departure. Here, however, we have a more traditional, even historic, architectural form landed on the roof as if it were a visitor from another age.

What is ironic as well, of course, is that the rooftop here is not one that hovers over the urban landscape but one that is tucked more discreetly beneath it; the glass facade of the office building looms above the rooftop. Nevertheless, building on the lowly garage rooftop is yet another way of putting the urban rooftop to use. Here is the case of the rooftop almost, but not quite, defining the building base. It is yet another reversal, this one of course, of the way we customarily imagine the roofscape.

Photographs: Courtesy of Shinkenchiku

Below Right *Shinto shrine, view from below*

Below Left *Rooftop Shinto shrine, detail*

Right *Rooftop Shinto shrine, side view*

Aceland
Oakland, California

Ace Architects
Oakland, California

The program called for the remodeling and expansion of three commercial buildings in downtown Oakland. Specifically, it meant the addition of three thousand square feet, a second floor and lobby to an existing commercial building that was set back from the street, as well as the remodeling of the facades of the adjacent one-story retail buildings.

The architects fulfilled the program—which they had dubbed Aceland—by creating a vocabulary of rooftop profiles. Or perhaps it was a case of picking up the diverse fragments of different vocabularies. Indeed, if the urban landscape of Oakland could be described as an eclectic mix of nondescript forms, this new vocabulary takes that eclecticism to a new and livelier extreme. These

are images that invigorate the cityscape and bring a new vibrance to the existing urban collage.

Although similar in spirit, the new rooftop profiles are distinct from one another in form and in material. Together they invent an identity for the nondescript storefronts. The larger, rear commercial building, with a travel agency at street level, was expanded through a rooftop addition—a second and third floor—with domes at both ends. The domes, in fact, accommodate offices, a mezzanine, and conference room. Constructed of silo tops positioned on block towers and surfaced in stucco, the pale blue domes suggest a Moroccan roofscape in downtown Oakland.

Using playful international imagery, the architects applied global references on a village scale: If the domes evoke a Middle Eastern aura, the rooftop profiles of the adjacent buildings are in sharp contrast. The yellow wooden towers and cornices of one building suggest early New England architecture, complete with awnings

---

Above *View of Aceland from street*

Left *Aceland after nightfall*

designed as overscaled dentils. Equally unpredictable is a red-painted brick building with Romanesque parapets and pilasters across the plaza; even its pair of curved glass and steel awnings slope up instead of down. As architect Lucia Howard concludes, "Though rendered in three separate vocabularies, the buildings are a collection of similar pieces. Each possesses a single symmetrical facade, with twin towers or parapets at either end. Yet each symmetrical elevation faces its own direction."

It is clear that the folly of these constructions is not limited to their rooftop imagery. Indeed, the three facades comprise a more complete program of the unexpected. English garden follies were not simply built curiosities intended to startle the unsuspecting wanderer; often they meant as well to serve a function, ranging from simply being a place to find solitude and repose to a place to bathe, fish, or even observe horse races. While the mosaic of building types in this renovation may not aspire to quite the same extravagance of whimsy, these follies are their urban counterpart, serving both to startle and amuse the onlooker while purposefully extending the commercial space of their conventional storefronts.

Below   *Aceland plaza, street view*

Above Right   *Aceland, detail of rooftop profile*

Below Right   *Aceland domes, exterior view*

Photographs: Alan Weintraub

GLASS HOUSES:
Laboratories for Light

Introduction

If rooftop acreage is located in the provinces of light and air, what building material would be more natural for its constructions than glass?

By nature, urban townhouses and apartments forego these commodities. Narrow building lots, the proximity of adjacent buildings, and the carving of apartment buildings into as many units as codes permit all contribute to that common idiom of urban living: a dark interior with few windows, and with the windows that there are revealing bleak vistas of air shafts and masonry walls.

Rooftop building is, of course, the grand exception to this rule. Although canyons of taller buildings may rise up around them, rooftop buildings, by definition, have clear setbacks that afford them abundant light, a commodity rare and precious in urban construction. By their nature, rooftop additions are more visually connected to adjacent rooftops and sky than they are to the street-level architecture that surrounds them; and the transparent, membrane walls of the glass house can exploit this connection almost effortlessly.

Glass is used in the construction of rooftop additions to illuminate and define not only the rooftop building: Often, interior stairwells and walls remain open as well to bring this natural light captured from the rooftop into the space below. A floor, or partial floor, constructed of glass block is another natural conduit for daylight. Building glass houses on the roof, then, is also a way of transferring volumes of light and spaciousness to the darker interiors below the roofline.

The trick, of course, may be in how these constructions are also able to negotiate privacy. For all its apparent fragility, glass is a versatile building material. Frosted glass or thick glass blocks can transmit light while limiting visibility. Simultaneously, a play between the transparent and translucent materials is created. As a means of partitioning space, such glass walls remain gracefully ambiguous. At once, they separate and connect. A glass wall functions as a veil between spaces, subtly suggesting the division of space rather than making the sterner division that the use of more substantial materials would create.

Living under glass also raises obvious safety questions. The occupants of glass aeries may feel visually, if not physically, vulnerable. Wired glass may work at least as a visual deterrent to intrusion. Glass walls may also be deliberately designed only for the more public areas of the house, while the more private zones are signaled by more substantial materials. And these differences between transparency and opacity may be used to define not only the various spaces of an interior but their functions as well.

For all the aesthetic or stylistic advantages of glass, it is also a practical material for rooftop building. Frequently, in older buildings especially, the structural plans for the existing building may not be available, and the rooftop architect has to consider the possibility that the base building may not be able to support the weight of concrete slab and brick masonry construction. A more lightweight material, glass, especially when used with steel or aluminum framing, may be the most practical way to add space without adding substantial weight. And the comparative low maintenance and cost make the appeal of glass construction even greater.

Recent advances in the technology of double glazing address the predictable problems of heating and cooling glass houses. The efficiency of double glazing is the result of a layer of air that is sandwiched between two layers of glass and works as insulation. While double glazing may not have the energy efficiency of a masonry wall, it does work as a buffer between interior and exterior temperatures, maintaining cooled temperatures at the height of summer or warm temperatures in winter.

For the sake of privacy and energy efficiency alike, shading mechanisms from the primitive to the ultra-automatic can be installed. Standard-issue blinds, curtains, and louvers serve the purpose, as do fiberglass and other synthetic mesh materials that can be stretched over the membrane of the glass surface to limit visibility and heat buildup while allowing light in.

These dazzling glass rooftop aeries can also serve as greenhouses, as plant life is the organic ornamentation they so obviously invite. The natural textures, colors, and patterns of the garden invigorate and warm the cooler technological components of the glass house. Such spaces blur the distinctions all the more between outside and in, shelter and open air—perceptual ambiguities that are unlikely and provocative in the contemporary urban environment.

Overleaf *Rudolph residence, exterior view*

Left *Rudolph residence, exterior evening view*

Layering With Light
New York, New York

Paul Rudolph, Architect
New York, New York

Most rooftop aeries seem to perch lightly on the solid ground of their rooftops as discrete observatories in the vast urban skyscape. The rooftop residence designed by Paul Rudolph for himself, however, bends and flows like a river of light, air, and greenery over and around the more solid and traditional painted brownstone of the row house beneath it. Rudolph's aerie doesn't so much crown the existing building as it quietly designates it as a neutral, elegant building base.

Rudolph's style of building transcends categories, but as a pupil of Walter Gropius and later, in the late fifties and early sixties, as Yale University's Dean of the School of Architecture, he became one of this country's most articulate speakers for the Modern Movement. His build-ings refined the cadences and modulated the idioms of modernism, often humanizing them in the process. Rudolph's own New York apartment carries this expression to a new precision and clarity.

Rudolph negotiates light the way other architects might work with more material elements. The architectural critic Michael Sorkin writes that "Architectural space is materialized by light. And no architect is more heliotropic than Rudolph. For him, light (like space) is substantial, sculptable. In his studies for projects Rudolph actually draws the light—not just according to conventions of shade/shadow but as a myriad of tiny arrows flowing through space, as if he could detect the photons with his pen." Indeed, in this apartment, the tiers of different spaces hover and float around a central, soaring living area. The precise planes of different areas seem to be interjected into this central space, but in a manner that seems to multiply space rather than divide it.

Left *Rudolph residence, interior terrace*

Above *Rudolph residence, exterior view*

115

Rudolph's scrupulous attendance to materials reflects the Bauhaus philosophy that architecture should be an intersection for art and crafts. The form, texture, and surface of all materials used in this interior play with transparency and translucence, with occasional jolts of opacity. Light mediates the furnishings, as well as the form, of Rudolph's residence; surface materials were specified to manipulate and modulate the light that defines the volumes of interior space. There are the beams laminated in stainless steel and floors of stainless steel and Plexiglas; shelves, cabinetry, tables and chairs are constructed in Plexiglas. Elsewhere, surfaces of glass, mirrors, stone, and even water all continue the spirited dialogue with light.

This rooftop does not tower over the adjacent buildings; rather, it seems to nestle comfortably as a light zone within the darker canyons of Manhattan. At night especially, it glitters as a nest of luminescence.

A series of terraces establish an interlude between the soaring residence and the less-ordered gridlock beneath it. Says Rudolph himself of the space: "The rooftop at Beekman Place enjoys its place in the sun, partially because a zone of space created by steel columns and beams supporting wisteria on trellises protects the inner space. This intermediate zone acts as a buffer between the interior spaces, the noisy city close by, and the brilliant sun overhead." Indeed, these terraces and intermediary layers work as an eloquent introduction to the precise, translucent splendors within.

Photographs: © Peter Aaron/ESTO

Below *Rudolph residence, dining area mezzanine over living area*

Right *Rudolph residence, exterior view*

117

A Modernist Greenhouse
New York, New York

Harry Stein, Untitled
Los Angeles, California

Harry Stein and his client, a film director, are both from Los Angeles. Says Stein of his client, "He wanted an openness and access to the outdoors not typically found in a Manhattan apartment." No surprise, then, that he chose to look for it on the open terrain of the rooftop.

The rooftop the client settled on was that of a one-hundred-year-old piano factory that had been converted to an apartment building in Manhattan's Hell's Kitchen neighborhood. The building itself was only six stories high, and other buildings in the immediate area were of a similar height; thus the rooftop offered open views of the city skyline and of the Hudson River to the west.

Above *Stein rooftop exterior against New York City skyline*

Left *Stein rooftop terrace overlooking midtown Manhattan*

Stein gutted and entirely reworked an existing small, two-bedroom penthouse. He stretched the space with a glass-and-steel framework that is strategically positioned between an existing parapet and the rooftop of the original penthouse. The new penthouse accommodates two living rooms, a dining area, kitchen, bedroom, and bath in a plan that balances the private areas of the house with the spacious, light-filled greenhouse structure that is more public. And while the whole penthouse measures twenty-five hundred square feet, the glass walls to the south and west, as well as a glass roof over the west-facing living room, suggest greater volumes of light and space. Curves are thrown to the neutral tones and furnishings of the space by pieces of sculpture, the sculptural forms of lighting fixtures and the stove, and the vibrant colors and textures of a small rug. It is an application of materials and textures that eloquently continues the classic modernist idiom.

Stein specified double glazing for the walls

and roof. He also installed a shading mechanism for the glass roof. Made of a fiberglass mesh, the system is activated automatically when the sunlight reaches a certain degree of intensity, or when the wind is especially strong.

Unlike most native New York architects, Stein operated on the premise that the outdoors is not a hostile environment, and he transformed the tar paper rooftop to a network of decks that serve as outdoor entertainment areas. Totalling approximately five thousand square feet, the various decks, sparse furniture, and assorted pieces of sculpture indeed shape usable space of the outdoors. A spiral steel staircase leads from the penthouse level to the observatory above the penthouse. Because the vistas from these various decks open onto neighboring rooftops of a similar height, treetops, and other diverse rooftop paraphernalia, there is the sense of residing in a village, with the grander city skyline ascending in the distance. There, the remote and peculiar silhouette of construction cranes poised on the skyscrapers' towers loom as accessories integral to the eccentric urban skyscape.

Photographs: Norman McGrath

Below   *Stein rooftop, floor plan*

Below   *Stein rooftop, living area*

Right   *Stein rooftop, dining area and terrace*

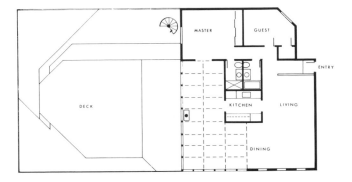

A Geometry of Translucence
New York, New York

William McDonough Architects
New York, New York

When the clients of New York City architect William McDonough purchased their loft on the top floor of the eleven-story, prewar office building in lower Manhattan that had been previously converted to an apartment building, it came with that nebulous term *roof rights.* And when they found that their first child was on the way, availing themselves of these roof rights appeared to be the obvious, if not only, way to get the necessary extra space.

In this case, however, the roof rights to the building totalled one thousand square feet of floor space, with two hundred and fifty square feet allotted to each of the four tenants occupying the top floor of the building. The two hundred and fifty square feet allotted to McDonough's

clients, aside from simply not being enough space, hardly justified the considerable costs of going through the roof. Only by negotiating with their neighbors to secure additional roof rights were McDonough's clients able to gain the necessary rooftop floor space.

McDonough, then a principal of the firm McDonough & Rainey, designed the new penthouse to accommodate a master bedroom suite, designed essentially as a double square, with the bedroom on one side and dressing room and bath on the other. "Structurally, we worked with what was there," he explains. "We like to work from a karate, rather than boxing, approach to things, and tried to run with the grain of the building. The stairs, for example, run between two beams in the existing roof, so we didn't have to resort to any draconian structural changes to install them."

Because the penthouse is sited on a semi-public roof—other occupants of the building have access to and are permitted to use the roof—

Above *McDonough rooftop, illuminated at night*

Left *McDonough rooftop, with view of Empire State Building*

maintaining privacy was of utmost concern. All the same, the clients wanted the penthouse to be filled with ample light that would filter down to the loft below as well. McDonough's solution was to install grids of sandblasted double glazing and a frieze of clerestories. All the lower panels of the double glazed glass have been frosted, while the upper panels remain clear, affording views of the copper cornices of an adjacent building as well as the silhouette of the more distant Empire State Building. The double-glazed units were all custom built, with only the interior panels sandblasted.

Painted white and filled with light, the penthouse is in marked contrast to the two-thousand-square-foot loft below, where tinted plaster has been used to reinforce the strong vertical planes of the space. "We like to think of walls as objects as well as surfaces," explains McDonough, referring to the frescoed walls and tinted pilasters of the loft. And indeed, the luminous grid of the penthouse works as a shimmering sculpture, in the evening hours especially, and expresses this philosophy with all the more eloquence.

Photographs: Frederick Charles

Below *McDonough rooftop, exterior view*

Bottom Right *Stairway leading to McDonough rooftop*

Top Right *McDonough rooftop, bedroom*

A Double-Glazed, Triple Decker
New York, New York

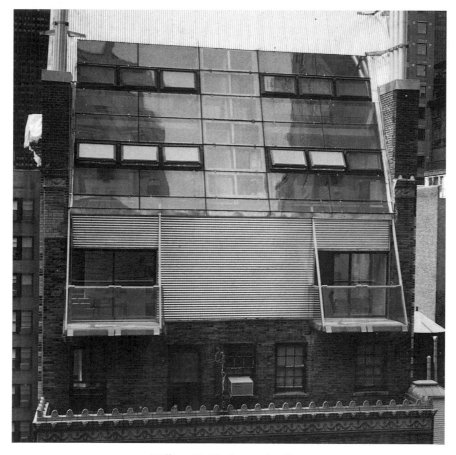

William B. Gleckman, Architect
New York, New York

"This was a building constructed in the twenties," explains architect William Gleckman, "that has served at various times as a hotel, bordello, and speakeasy." And while its current incarnation as an apartment building may be less colorful, Gleckman's rooftop addition lives up to its spirited past.

Gleckman has constructed two triplex apartments by entirely gutting and renovating the fourteenth story, adding a new fifteenth story on the rooftop level, and installing a penthouse level above that. In doing so, he limited his use of materials to stainless steel and glass for two reasons. The first is that the uppermost reaches of the building afford glimpses of Central Park, and these are materials that exploit the light and view of high-altitude architecture.

The second and perhaps more important reason for his choice had do do with the material at-

tributes of stainless steel and glass. Whereas masonry and concrete add substantial weight to a building, stainless steel and glass are more lightweight and put less strain on the building. "Because this sixty-five-year old building had a steel frame for which no plans were available," explains Gleckman, "it was absolutely necessary to select the lightest possible construction materials." He also describes stainless steel and glass as "inert" materials that are low cost and maintenance free.

Gleckman points out that this building, as well as many of New York City's pre-twenties buildings, had had its rooftop paved with "promenade tiles,"— quarry tiles that were intended to transform the rooftop into a usable terrace. Invariably, however, the tile would later leak. The customary procedure was then to cover the whole roof with a layer of roofing paper, and to patch leaks as they constantly reappeared. "I urge my clients to just rip it all up," admits Gleckman. "A far more efficient and productive solution would be to construct sloping glass-and-

---

Left and Above *Gleckman rooftop, exterior view*

stainless-steel roofs which immediately drain and get rid of the water as well as providing usable, rentable, or saleable space."

Gleckman's system for the rooftop enclosure is one he invented himself. The system is made up of components: glass sheets, stainless steel clips, tape, and a sealer, all of which "fit together like the pieces of an erector set." It is a system of butt-glazing that bypasses the frames traditionally used in the construction of glass curtain walls. Instead, sheets of insulated, tempered glass are secured to the lightweight steel structure by stainless steel clips. The glass panels were butt-glazed, using an English tape called Emseal, which was then protected on the exterior with a sealant to prevent leaks. "Frames collect water and eventually lead to leaks," says Gleckman, "which is why they're impractical for rooftop building." On this particular building, two front balconies at the fourteenth story have been constructed of structural stainless steel and continue the sloping lines of the facade.

Gleckman concludes that "the new superstructure represents a new cap built with today's materials and technology. It differs completely in texture and design from the existing building of the 1920s and yet, in my opinion, is strangely suitable without trying in any way to emulate the spirit of the old." Indeed, while Gleckman's addition is a radical departure from the vernacular of the existing structure, its contemporary language is a way of making a rundown rooftop a functional, practical space.

Photographs: William Gleckman

Below and Right   *Gleckman rooftop plans*

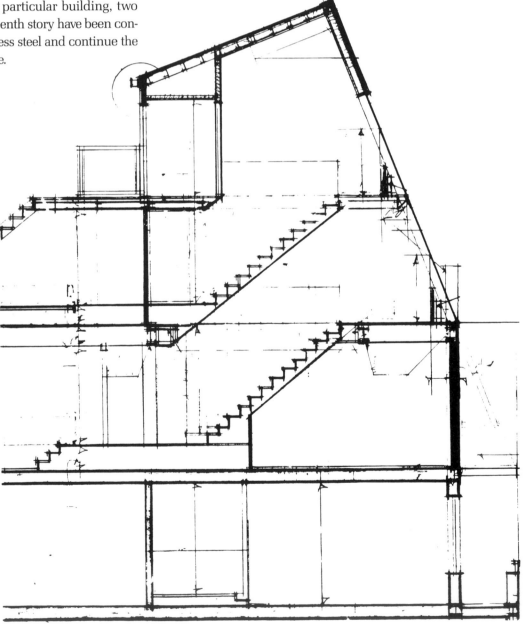

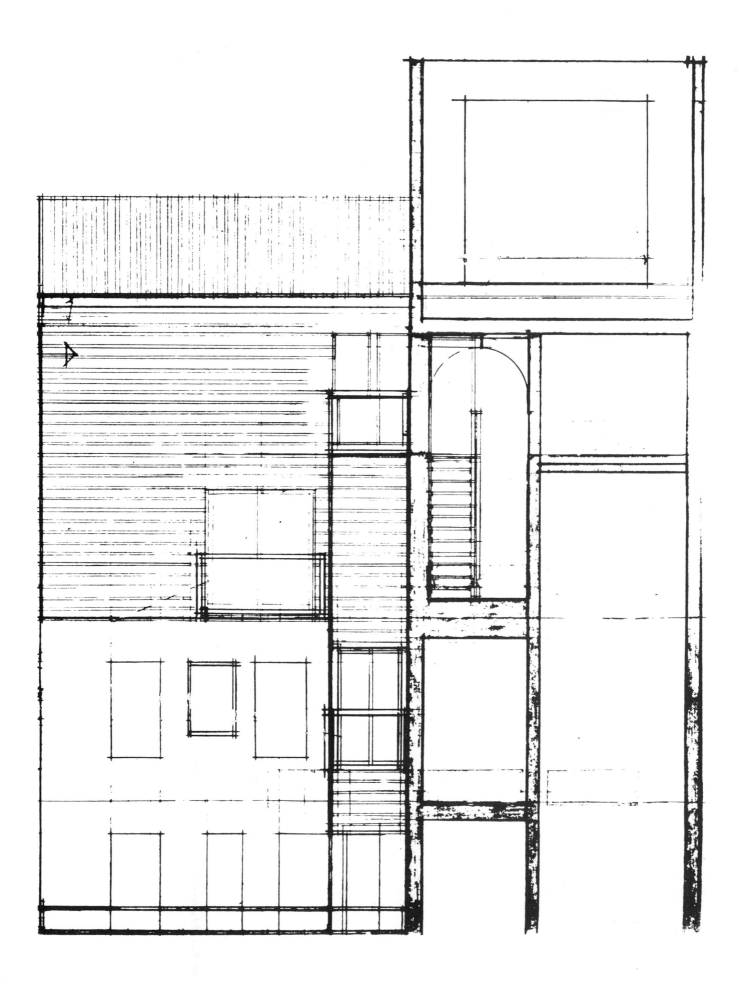

An Urban Observatory
New York, New York

Peix & Crawford
New York, New York

Architect Doug Peix describes this rooftop addition as "a 'Piano Nobile' living room, an urban observatory from which the starry nights and constellations of city light can be enjoyed." And indeed, an expansive skylight—twenty by twenty-six feet—has been transformed into a formal living room that hovers above the rest of the apartment, not unlike the formal reception area of Renaissance architecture. Perched on a relatively low, five-story industrial building, the expansive proportions of the skylight suggest spaciousness and volume, if not actual height.

Originally illuminating a light-industrial commercial shop, the immense skylight had a ridge line twenty-six feet above the main floor level. When Peix's client purchased the space, however,

he converted it to a residence with two bedrooms, a dining/kitchen area, and bath. The extra space made available through the unusual height of the ridge line persuaded him to create a second floor level, which, measuring four hundred square feet, became the glass-encased living room.

The skylight itself was totally reglazed with wired glass—selected both as a safety measure and for its industrial aesthetic quality, which correlated with the nature of the building. Although the bulk of the glazing was northfacing, the budget dictated singleglazing and made for unusal heating and cooling requirements. "The first summer our client lived there," Peix recalls, "he had an enormous, six-foot cactus in the living room. It wilted." Peix's design specified that the lower level of frosted windows could be opened. With the aid of a ceiling fan and an industrial exhaust fan, these windows allow cooler air to circulate in the summer. In the winter, the space is heated through units encircling the base of the room,

---

Above *Peix skylight addition at twilight*

Left *Peix skylight addition, interior view*

131

supplemented by a pot-bellied stove. Peix explains that the somewhat complicated configuration of the skylight would have made a shading system a difficult, not to mention costly, proposition. "Besides," he adds, "the client didn't want to use any materials that would compromise all that glass."

Because most of the adjacent buildings are of a similar height, visual privacy was not a critical issue. All the same, Peix's client did share rooftop access with several other residents of the building. Because the living room floor is below the baseline of the roof, the frosted glass windows at the base of the skylight maintain sufficient distance and privacy. The client's own access to the roof is via the gabled doorway, Peix's only structural addition to the skylight.

The staircase leading to the kitchen and dining room below has been left open, and with a square landing at its base, it suggests a sense of formality. Together with the railings at one end of the living room, the open staircase allows daylight to stream through the area below.

Photographs: Robert Perron

ADAPTIVE REUSE:

When Restorations and Renovations Go Through The Roof

Introduction

Historic preservation is gaining a foothold in contemporary urban design and planning. In the last twenty years, the reuse and recycling of old buildings has become nearly as critical to successful urban planning as the design and construction of new ones. Rooftop additions can be a vital part of such reuse agendas.

Two major factors are behind the gaining momentum of the preservation movement. First, there is the growing public recognition that recycling older buildings salvages not only buildings but very real fragments of urban history and culture. Enriched by their history, such buildings give us a cultural perspective and a sense of physical location in the continuum of time.

Preservation of buildings has all the more value at a time when public enthusiasm for modern and postmodern architecture is at a low ebb. The purported functionalism on which modernism was founded placed little value on the decorative idiosyncracies of preceding historic styles. For all its good intentions, the corporate translation of modernism in this country was frequently a clinical affair of steel and glass. Indeed, the visual sterility and overall mediocrity of much watered-down "modern" architecture has fueled the preservation movement.

The second factor contributing to the momentum of the current preservation movement is a part of the legislation known as the 1976 Tax Reform Act, which provides economic incentives in the form of tax abatements to builders and developers willing to invest in a slice of architectural history. In practical terms this means developers and builders may have a substantial financial interest not only in restoring old buildings, but in recycling them to serve contemporary needs.

Such restorations indeed test the imagination of all involved. Ultimately it is their incongruity that engages the human spirit. It is clearly contradictory for one to dine in a rehabilited bank or have cocktails in a post office. These buildings were constructed to serve specific functions, and deviations from them appeal to our sense of humor; they provoke our curiosity and foster a sense of intrigue. As creative as it may be to transform a railway station's waiting room into an elegant restaurant, it is also a departure from conventional wisdoms that determine certain buildings will serve certain functions.

Eccentricities of the human spirit, of course, embrace such departures. Here, of course, is where rooftop additions come into the picture. Rooftop additions are often pursuits in architectural incongruity. When coupled with a preservation project that has already radically altered the function of an older building, a rooftop addition can be the crowning achievement of built caprice.

Yet rooftop additions to older buildings also have a more practical side. Many older buildings—those built before World War II—were not constucted to the maximum density permitted by the zoning and building codes established later. Also, such buildings, while perhaps underbuilt in terms of height, may have been overbuilt in terms of structure and support. The steel beams that support the rooftops of many of these buildings may also support the additional weight of a rooftop construction. If a building is to be renovated, either for its historic significance or for the tax abatements that reward such preservation efforts, than these two factors can also render such a building an ideal contender for rooftop construction.

In incorporating a rooftop addition to the adaptive reuse of an entire building, the architect can choose one of two options: The addition can be sympathetic to the existing building, taking its design cues from what has already been established. Or, in its use of modern materials, construction and embellishment, it can establish a contrast to the older building below. Obviously, the historic value of the existing building may be the foremost consideration in determining which of these options is most appropriate.

The projects shown on the following pages demonstrate the validity of both approaches, but what ties them all together is their scale. These are corporate or commercial rooftop additions that are larger in scope than many of the other additions shown in this book. The point they so eloquently make is that rooftop additions need not be limited to the roof rights of an individual resident tenant. Rather than simply enlarging the living space of a single city apartment, rooftop additions can also increase significantly the commercial space and value of existing, older buildings. And in doing so, they become part of more ambitious, more expensive, and altogether grander preservation programs.

Overleaf *The NBBJ Group rooftop lunchroom at dusk*

Left *Helene Curtis Headquarters*

A Collage Of Classicism
Washington, D.C.

Shalom Baranes Associates, Architects
Washington, D.C.

To date, Washington, D.C. has put into effect one of this country's most stringent preservation programs, one that makes it virtually impossible to demolish historically significant buildings. The city also has an eleven-story height limit that further maintains its old world architectural flavor of wide boulevards, broad vistas, and low buildings. Inevitably, though, the antiquated design and layout of many of the city's older buildings may prevent them from being economic or functional spaces, thus undermining any contemporary usefulness or relevance. In the renovations of such buildings, retaining the facade, while reconfiguring the interior and adding space on the rooftop, is one practical design resolution that is sympathetic to the goals of preservation. In-

deed, that rooftop construction can be integral to the rehabilitation of historically significant buildings has been consistently put to test in the nation's capital by architect Shalom Baranes.

"The emergence of facade retention as an acceptable preservation solution in Washington, D.C. is a reflection of both the strength and quality of the local preservation community as well as the general public's crisis of confidence in Modern Architecture," writes Baranes. (Shalom Baranes, "The Architectural Perspective: Preservation and Development," *Realtor*, April, 1984, p.14) And indeed, the architect has built his reputation on renovations that are fine-tuned, deferential to the architecture of the existing building and that take their design cues from it.

A case in point is the Bond Building. Only one block from the White House, this office building had nevertheless fallen into disrepair and for years had been boarded up. But with an ornate beaux arts facade, preservationists raised an out-

---

Above *The Bond Building, construction view*

Below *The Bond Building, exterior view*

cry when demolition was suggested. Baranes's ultimate rehabilitation program for the building restored the facade and added a seventy thousand square foot, four-story rooftop addition, all of which nearly doubled the square footage of the existing seven-floor building. It was a restoration agenda that maintained, indeed continued, the visual rhythms and proportions of the building.

Baranes's four-story addition is a layer that fuses old with new in a collage of classical decorative detailing. The base of the building, with a facade of carved, cream colored Italian marble, was faithfully restored, with the architects referring to old photographs of the original designs. The facade of the existing upper floors, a combination of brick and stone, was cleaned and repaired, and some sections were replaced. Windows were replaced, although the original wood frames were salvaged.

Baranes used materials that matched those of the existing building for the rooftop addition, although he took liberties with the original patterns and decoration. The most notable of these

liberties is the glazed area, in the form of ribbon windows, behind the row of paired columns on both facades. While such a design scheme may not be consistent with beaux arts aesthetics, it is a layering that seems oddly sympathetic to the confection of classical revival ornament below.

Photographs: Walter Smalling, Jr.

Below *The Bond Building, floor plan*

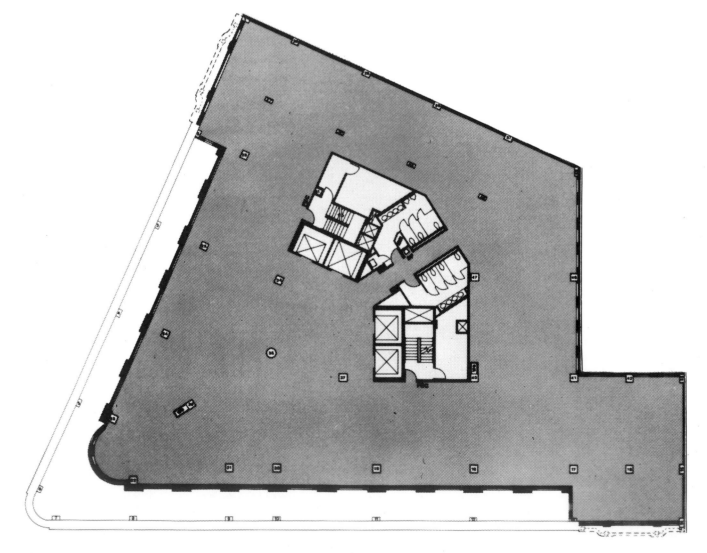

Adding A Layer Of History
Washington, D.C.

Shalom Baranes Associates, Architects
Washington, D.C.

Washington, D.C.'s Southern Building was designed by D. H. Burnham in 1911. The original plans were drawn up for an eleven-story building, but the developer's financial setbacks restricted actual construction to nine stories. All this was very much to the point some seventy-two years later when controversy arose regarding the possible expansion of the office building. Indeed, while the original architectural plans for the two unbuilt floors were never located, both documentation of the intent to build and a set of structural drawings that revealed the base, footprint, and height of the additional two floors were available. More important, perhaps, and what ultimately silenced the controversy, was the fact that the building accommodated steel columns and beams sufficient to support the weight of two extra floors.

Architect Shalom Baranes worked with Burnham's successor firm, Graham Anderson Probst & White, and with architectural historian Betty Bird. Not surprisingly, then, his rooftop addition, while adding close to thirty-two thousand square feet of new space, also defers courteously to the existing design; while going up in height, it goes back in time. Like the building itself, the addition has been constructed in a creamy terra cotta and brick—although, inevitably, the new is slightly brighter than the old.

Burnham's original design included an elaborate terra cotta cornice that projected three feet out over the building. "What made this project so interesting," observes Baranes, "is that we didn't know initially whether the cornice was meant to be at the building's roofline, or below the additional two floors." While the roof and existing penthouse were removed altogether, the cornice remained in place, although sections of it were repaired.

Above *The Southern Building, construction view*

141

Baranes's addition would appear less seamless if the facade of the original building had not been so carefully restored. The new facade includes new storefronts at the street level that do not replicate the original configurations. Rather, the original heavy wood frames were replaced by slimmer bronze framing more consistent with a contemporary upscale retail image. The upper floors of office space, however, were restored more faithfully. New double-glazed and double-hung windows have replaced the originals, while the damaged terra cotta ornamentation has been repaired or replaced.

In its simplicity, Baranes's addition does nothing to distract attention from the original ornamentation. Rather, by following the established patterns, proportion, and general visual rhythms of the building, the architect has completed the building in a manner very close to its original plans—all the while bringing it functionally more up-to-date.

Photographs: Walter Smalling, Jr.

Left   *The Southern Building, exterior view*

Below   *The Southern Building before rooftop addition*

A Corporate Makeover
Chicago, Illinois

Booth/Hansen & Associates
Chicago, Illinois

Although Helene Curtis Industries may be better known for the cosmetic makeovers that transfigure its human clients, the renovation of the building that was to become its corporate headquarters in Chicago was as sublime a transformation as any that occur inside its salons. While the 1914 brick warehouse had relatively little historic value, its site on the Chicago River, the tax abatements available through renovating a building that was over fifty years old, and its location on the Chicago Loop all made the building an appealing choice for the company's headquarters.

The architects of Booth/Hansen & Associates modulated and refined the classical style of the existing building in their renovation to accommo-

date a more modern executive office landscape. The architects adopted the idea of an urban grid for their renovation. Conference rooms at the center of each floor suggest public plazas, while a perimeter of private offices suggests a downtown area. Hallways suggest urban avenues. Columns with exaggerated capitals suggest a skyline while also accommodating lighting and wire management.

A separate penthouse constructed on the roof adds further to usable office space. The penthouse, if the addition could indeed be called that, occupies the entire roof, thereby adding approximately fourteen thousand, five hundred square feet of space—specifically an oval-shaped conference room flanked by executive offices and smaller meeting rooms. As project architect William Ketcham explains, "The existing building was underbuilt so there were no setback restrictions. We could have added as many as three stories."

Left and Above *Helene Curtis Headquarters*

The penthouse facade of triple-glazed, tinted windows ascends from the more solid brick mass of the existing building. And while the curtain-wall construction is indeed a deviation from the original masonry, the proportions of the new penthouse coincide with those of the original building, while its lines echo the classical symmetry and formalism of the building beneath.

Inside, in marked contrast to its modernist "glass box" facade, the boardroom conforms to a more classical plan. A simple row of columns outlines the perimeter of the boardroom and reasserts the curve of the glazed facade. In the double-height, somewhat grand boardroom itself, pilasters both evoke the columns used on the floors below and confer their own stately corporate aura. Lighting, from clerestory windows and a cove ceiling, remains soft and diffused.

Photographs: Hedrick-Blessing/Nick Merrick

A Corporate Conservatory

Seattle, Washington

The NBBJ Group, Architects
Seattle, Washington

Constructed in 1904, the five-story Heritage Building in downtown Seattle followed a graceful stylistic formula established by nineteenth-century Chicago architects. Its sandstone facade was composed of a ground floor that establishes a solid visual foundation. Above it were three intermediate floors with more expansive horizontal bands of windows. The fifth and top floor had smaller windows and more ornamental detailing. While it was listed on the National Register of Historic Places as part of Seattle's Pioneer Square Preservation District, the building had been demoted to warehouse status in recent years and was an open invitation for adaptive reuse. When the NBBJ Group of architects and environmental professionals undertook renovation of the building to

serve as its own headquarters in 1982, the building's landmark status was not limited to historic preservation. In its sensitive balancing act of nostalgia with contemporary urban needs, it is also a landmark in the more recent development of adaptive reuse.

As Patrick James of NBBJ has noted, "Historic preservation can embalm or reinvigorate." This, clearly, is a case of the latter. The exterior of the mixed-use building has remained largely intact, although the sandstone facade was acid-cleaned, the fenestration repaired and a new entrance added. The expansive interior, on the other hand, has been revamped entirely to accommodate over twelve thousand feet of retail space for a furniture store on street level, as well as over sixty thousand square feet of office space on the upper floors for NBBJ's 235-member staff. While some of the interior's original brick and timber construction remains exposed, its textures are juxtaposed throughout by the sleek white partitioning

---

Left and Above *The NBBJ Group rooftop lunchroom, exterior view*

used elsewhere in the largely open plan. A central open staircase, illuminated by a vast skylight overhead, is the visual and functional focus. The open stairs have balconies at every floor to reinforce a sense of visibility and communication.

The crowning achievement of the restoration is, of course, the new penthouse. Accessed through both elevators and an interior staircase, the penthouse is used as an employee lounge and lunchroom. The glazed, two-thousand-square-foot pavilion opens onto an open deck that further increases usable roof space. Constructed of white-painted steel and glass with a wood floor, the penthouse pavilion can be ventilated in warm seasons through electrically operable windows at the peak. During winter months, the pavilion is solar heated. Its setback prevents the penthouse from being visible at street level, thereby preserving the existing streetscape. The setback is a statement of modesty and restraint appropriate to—but all too often lacking in—such historic renovations.

With its panoramic view of the city, Puget Sound and the Olympic Mountains, the penthouse also functions as a starlit aerie for evening parties and receptions. With its form and materials suggesting a classical conservatory, the penthouse has historic evocations that are appropriate and sensitive to this restoration.

Photographs: Dick Busher

Below *The NBBJ Group headquarters, elevation drawing*

Right *The NBBJ Group rooftop lunchroom, interior view*

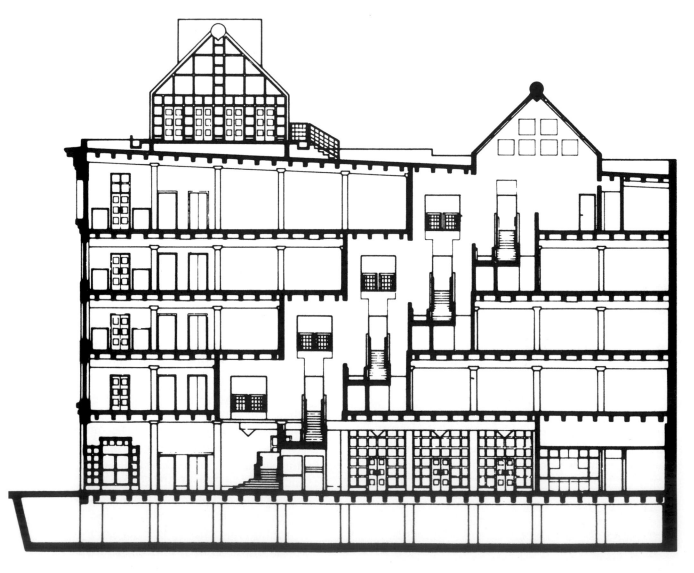

TEMPLES AT THE TOP:

Unlikely Marriages of Neo-Classicism and Blacktop

Introduction

If incongruity is one of the keynotes of rooftop architecture, what style could better suit rooftop constructions than neoclassicism? What could seem more out of place than a small, serene Greek temple floating above the frenzied arteries of the modern metropolis? But in architecture, as in life, it is the unpredictable, unusual, and entirely unlikely marriages that are often the happiest. Indeed, the meeting of blacktop and neoclassicism can result in the sublime. That such templelike structures should find their way to city rooftops is, of course, altogether natural, for the modern urban environment is surely the place where they are most urgently needed.

To be sure, the neoclassical vocabulary is a staple of urban architecture. If classical architecture evokes qualities of somber grandeur and tranquility, then the builders of civic architecture at large have relied on this style of building not only for the solemnity it might confer on the building, but for the dignity it could presumably confer on the activities occurring inside as well. The stone pillars indigenous to the porticos of civic architecture everywhere uphold not simply the building's pediment and roof but the very values of righteousness, truth, and honor themselves.

Indeed, so much do we associate neoclassical architecture with grand buildings serving the public good that its adaptation to less sublime rooftop cottages inevitably provokes a response that here, certainly, is a folly. To be sure, the moral symbolism of such architecture may not be terribly significant to the architects and occupants of rooftops. All the same, classical elements do evoke the sense of solitude and repose that have increasingly become vital ingredients to rational urban life.

Left *Smith and Thompson listening room, facade and garden*

Overleaf *Machado-Silvetti terrace, view from above*

Blacktop And Baroque
New York, New York

Smith and Thompson Architects
New York, New York

Its substantial setback prevents this rooftop addition to a brownstone in New York City designed by Smith and Thompson Architects from being visible from the street below and from disrupting the semibaroque facade of the brownstone. From the West Side Highway twenty blocks away, however, the addition appears something like a small Greek temple hovering in miraculous repose above a row of brownstones.

This quality of serenity infuses the interior of the rooftop addition as well. Designed for a music critic, the sixteen-by-twenty-foot room was intended to function primarily as a listening laboratory that also accommodated a massive record collection and stereo equipment. It is described by Smith as being "an interface be-

tween the contemporary desire for the outdoors with light, air, and gardens, overlaid with an historical context." Indeed, it is a small, high room, a tranquil retreat designed as a large vault with two intersecting dormers. Standard sheetrock and a wood floor, not to mention the shelves upon shelves of books and records, make for good acoustics.

French doors on the north and south sides lead to wood deck terraces. The steps from the terrace on the north side lead down to the remaining northern half of the roof, which has been transformed—via plantings, redwood seating, and steel pipe railing—to a rooftop garden.

While a serene Greek temple might be an unusual structure to encounter on a Manhattan rooftop, the rooftop landscape of that particular Upper West Side block was already somewhat disparate. The row of brownstones to one side include not only the conventional array of pipes, chimneys, and stack vents, but a solar collector

---

Left *Terrace behind the Smith and Thompson listening room.*

Above *Smith and Thompson listening room, exterior*

as well. On the other side was a larger fifties apartment. Smith compares the more general sense of Manhattan's roofscapes to the rolling terrain of Italian hill towns and finds that the varying level of the rooflines is not unlike their "meandering hills and winding streets." And indeed, being remote from both the urban clamor below and the relentless grid of city blocks, this neoclassical listening room confirms that sense.

Photographs: Norman McGrath

Downscaled Formalism
New York, New York

Haverson/Rockwell
New York, New York

The columns and formal classical pediment framing the French doors at the entrance to architect David Rockwell's rooftop apartment not only add a sense of drama to the entryway, but also serve a more mundane function peculiar to rooftops: They conceal the exterior pipes of the eleven-story, 1920s New York City apartment building.

Constructed to be five maids' rooms, the original rooftop structure was a steel structure measuring approximately four hundred square feet. With his partner, Jay M. Haverson, Rockwell enlarged the space to seven hundred square feet, though keeping the original columns and roof and staying within the column spacing. The architects used classical elements indoors as well as out to give the apartment a greater sense of volume and

spaciousness. Formal classical details—the fireplace mantle and moldings, for example—were installed, but on a smaller scale than what is customary. And the cove ceilings, while adding a sense of volume to the small space, were actually installed to conceal the steel beams supporting the structure.

As with other rooftop additions, this apartment is surrounded by open space and light. "Where else could you install eleven French doors in a seven-hundred square-foot space?" questions Rockwell. To amplify that sense of light, the architects relied on several different devices. Rather than installing doors that would separate and close up the space, they shifted floor levels and materials to signify the different functions of different areas. The Santa Fe tile used in the living room is a shift from the wood used elsewhere and suggests a sense of transition.

The architects also specified warm quartz lighting, which is as close as artificial light can

---

Above *Rockwell residence, rooftop view*

Left *Rockwell residence, neoclassical facade*

come to natural daylight. Built-in furniture and storage areas keep clutter to a minimum and, along with wicker furniture, maintain a sense of lightness. A quarry tile floor and stone top table further suggest outdoor furniture and add to the ambiguity of indoors and out, which was the architects' primary intent. "Actually, it feels something like a beach house up there," muses Rockwell.

Or it comes as close to a beach house as it could using such a formal classical entrance. The formal pediment and columns have been constructed of light-gauge steel framing sheathed in plywood, which was then covered in a cement-like material called Sto. With a plaster or stucco-like finish, this material also has insulating properties. For outdoor furniture, the wrought iron garden chairs have been positioned in stylistic juxtaposition to the more formal columns and pediment.

Photographs: Paul Warchol

Below Left *Rockwell residence, bath*

Below Right *Rockwell residence, dining area*

Right *Rockwell residence, living area*

162

Classical Lattice
New York, New York

Machado and Silvetti Associates, Inc.
Boston, Massachusetts

Like the upper floors of so many Manhattan townhouses, those of this French neoclassical townhouse were originally intended to house servants and children. The terrace rooms subsequently designed by Boston architects Rodolpho Machado and Jorge Silvetti not only enlarge the usable penthouse space but expand on the idea of the outdoor room. While such rooms may be a staple of architecture of warmer climates, in New York City the use of outdoor space is conventionally centered around terrace gardens and imaginative applications of plant life. The design of these "rooms" is a more architectural treatment of the terrace that introduces an unconventional elegance to the rooftop.

Daylight filters through the sequence of the two outdoor rooms, one complete with a mock fireplace, through lattice walls that both articulate the rooms and make them transparent. And while the lattice walls, of course, do suggest a garden as well, the precise white trim persists that this is a more formal and traditional interior. The architects specified a blue green for the lattice walls, not necessarily for its cool, garden hues, but because it echoes the color of the building's copper mansard. The proportions and architectural details together suggest the serene order and dignity of classical architecture. Yet it is a lighthearted translation that is in keeping with the spirit of the rooftop region. The rooms float somewhere between indoors and out, between a private and serene garden and a proper drawing room. That such tranquility hovers above the urban clamor only adds to its ambiguity.

Photographs: Norman McGrath

Left *Machado-Silvetti terrace, dining area*

Above *Machado-Silvetti terrace, lattice walls*

ROOMS AT THE TOP:
Punctuating the Roofline

Introduction

While vacant stretches of blacktop terrain may often seem to invite expansive rooftop additions, the obstacles to building on the roof are themselves extensive. Foremost perhaps, is that most rooftops are not designed to support the weight of rooftop structures or the large gatherings such structures might eventually lead to; and reinforcing them to withstand such loads may be prohibitively expensive. Also, local zoning ordinances often prevent rooftop additions that would add to the square footage of floor space of the existing building. Finally, questions of egress and fire codes may make building at the rooftop level impractical. Working around such constraints, however, comes naturally to many urban architects, and those who design rooftop additions have found ways to venture onto the roof while keeping the restrictions in mind.

Single rooms, walkways, and even a small space barely more than an expanded skylight can puncture the roofline to create abbreviated urban observatories and bring volumes of light and space into the building below.

Overleaf   *The sky room*

Left   *The sky room, exterior view*

A Library Aerie
New York, New York

Smith-Miller + Hawkinson Architects
New York, New York

For his client, a painter, architect Henry Smith-Miller had originally designed the rooftop addition to a seven-story loft building in New York City's Soho as a studio with north-facing skylights. Local zoning ordinances, however, prevented the architect from adding floor space to the existing building. Unfazed, the architect then amended—or rather abbreviated—his plan and turned the addition into a skylight pavilion that induces light and sky into the loft. But it is a skylight through which one can walk, and one that is lined with shelves—a floating pavilion that doubles as a library. This is an addition, then, that provides not only a gateway to the landscape of the roof, but a metaphorical access to the literary zones one might find resting on its shelves. Its reduced dimensions, about one hundred square feet, also make for a private retreat, not the norm in the customary open loft.

"Architects in New York City so rarely get the chance to build houses. This was a rare opportunity to do an exterior, a pavilion," explains Smith-Miller. The structure, a metal and glass grid with exposed truss work, is indeed an aerie, a floating habitat. A corrugated tin exterior corresponds to the rooftop vernacular elsewhere in what was once an industrial district. And while the visual effect of metal and glass is one of openness and accessibility, they are actually impenetrable.

Urban density necessitates that existing buildings be continually examined for how they can best continue to be used. "The existing building is always being revised in different ways," says Smith-Miller. "And certainly the use of the rooftop will be ever increasing." That in mind, when and if local zoning changes, so too will what is on this rooftop.

Above *Stairway leading to the Smith-Miller sky library*

Left *The sky room, interior view*

Photographs: Adam Bartos

A Sky Room
San Francisco, California

Paulett Taggart Architects
San Francisco, California

The quality of light in the hills of San Francisco, the color of the bay, and the stucco facades of its buildings are often described as *Aegean* or *Mediterranean.* Unfortunately, however, other shared regional characteristics include steep, narrow, and increasingly precious building lots that make it all the more difficult to bring this light indoors.

A small rooftop addition designed by Paulett Taggart Architects in San Francisco for a three-story house on Telegraph Hill, however, does exactly that. As part of an overall renovation undertaken to make a single house out of two existing flats, the sky room was designed, among other reasons, as a means to illuminate the new house. As Taggert explains, "A problem typical of the San Francisco residence was the long building with light at both ends, but built to the property line at both sides and therefore with no light at the middle. The problem provided the opportunity for the creation of a dynamic vertical 'stairspace.' The light from the two clerestories and the sky room over the stair draw you up as you enter the house and balance the light for all of the rooms in the house."

Measuring ten by twelve feet, the sky room has only enough room for a built-in couch and two chairs. Nevertheless, it rises serenely above the building's horizontal roofline somewhat like a contemporary widow's walk. Despite its reduced scale, the addition both expands the usable living area of the residence and works as a light well. Light is drawn into the second and third floors through the open central stairway of perforated metal risers. Vertical cutouts along the stairway and glass block walls filter light to the interior and thereby integrate the three levels of the resi-

---

Above *The sky room, interior with built-in couch*

Left *The sky room, exterior view*

173

dence. The sky room itself and its adjacent deck function as a private retreat, but one offering expansive views of both city and bay.

Photographs: Jane Lidz

Below *The sky room, sectional perspective drawing*

Right *The sky room interior and exterior*

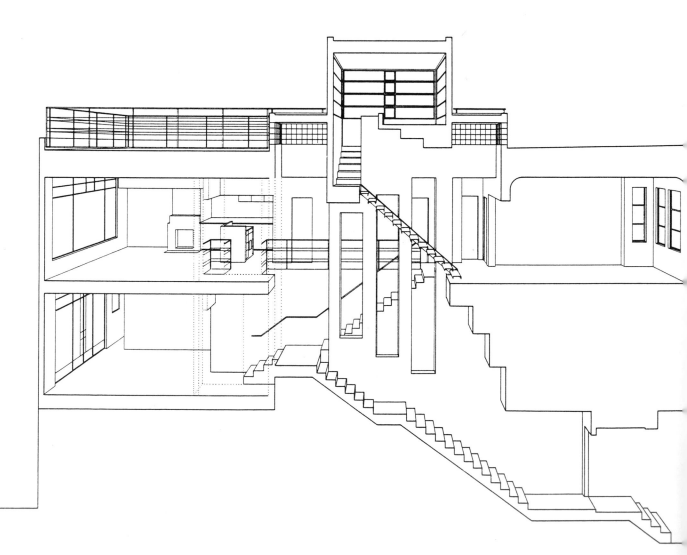

LAST THOUGHTS ON ADDING UP:

The Rooftop as a Design Workshop

As the additions shown on the previous pages indicate, the rooftop is the landscape of invention. And as one might suspect of such landscapes, their geography is not limited to urban areas. Nor are their inventions limited to constructions of the built world. If we consider the rooftop not simply as a vacant building plot, but as an ideological design workshop, then we might find an even broader range of rooftop constructions. Shown on these pages are some of these inventions, some built, some unbuilt, and many of them in the country, where a very different set of references govern design and construction. All the same, elements of their design and construction could be adapted to the urban rooftop.

Going through the roof may be an act that is carried out with the greatest vigor in urban areas. Because city rooftops may be the only unbuilt plots available to young architects, the energy and innovation that accompany such projects know few restraints. All the same, architects and design-

---

Overleaf *A rooftop frame. Photograph courtesy of Karen Bussolini*

Left and Below *Nantucket houses with widow's walks. Photos courtesy of Jenny Shakespeare, Design Assoc.*

---

ers seem equally destined and happy to go through the roof of country houses. These projects occupy a different site from their urban counterparts. Far from the grimy frontier of blacktop, rural rooftops begin with a more fluid, varied, and altogether eclectic set of components. Pitched roofs, gables, dormers, balconies, gingerbread ornamentation, and chimney pots alongside an infinity of other architectural elements can compose the more idiosyncratic roofline of rural houses. Who could argue that Shingle-style cottages, Victorian extravaganzas, Carpenter Gothic houses, even proper old New England farmhouses, barns, and silos all breed their own stylistic eccentricities? Consider the widow's walk, that eccentricity of what is usually more somber New England architecture. While the function of these fanciful rooftop deviations remains open to question, that they are a spirited deviation from the more regimented design of the stately houses beneath them is clear. Understandably, then, rather than being the visually incongruous follies that seem to blossom inexplicably from the desert blacktop, rooftop additions to country houses may be more in sync with an already eccentric roofline. At times, too, these additions may be visual references to more eclec-

tic architectural elements beneath them.

Consider the proposed Moon Porch designed by Atlanta architect James Mount for a house in Vidalia, Georgia. Rather than using urban blacktop and its various appendages as a springboard, Mount used more regional references, conceiving of this rooftop observatory as an architectural foil to the more traditional sun porch. "The porch," he says, "as in all good southern residential architecture, protects visitors and owners from the harsh sun." Mount has taken this regional standard and renegotiated it for the rooftop of this 3,000-square-foot family home in Georgia.

The house itself lies at the end of a long, pine-shaded driveway that winds through the pastures of a former horse farm. The sun porch, skewed at an angle from the main house and located at its entry, is also designed to greet visitors. The Moon Porch, however, should it be built, might be perceived more as a terminus than a point of entry; and moonlight hardly demands that its viewers be protected or shaded. This rooftop porch, then, forty feet above the ground and at the opposite end of the house from the sun porch, was designed more as an evening observatory. Its access is through an interior family room, although the steep stairway on the facade could

serve as an access as well. Built of heart redwood—as the house itself is—the porch transcends the flat roof of the house like an exotic, tropical interpretation of a widow's walk. The large oculus inserted at its peak echoes a similar window on the sun porch below.

With its steeply stepped facade and temple-like structure at its summit, the Moon Porch is also reminiscent of Aztec temples. Mount then, has taken several recognizable idioms of tropical architecture—structures that are designed with the heat, the intense light, and even the spiritual and religious powers of the sun in mind—and translated them to address the more subtle atmosphere suggested by the moon.

Mount has hardly limited his design vocabulary to regional references in a rooftop addition in Santa Rosa Beach, Florida that *was built.* The forms he has adapted in this idiosyncratic roofline represent a cultural and historical exchange program, a graceful collision of the ancient and the modern. The structure recalls at

Right *Moon Porch, model*

Below *Moon Porch, working drawings*

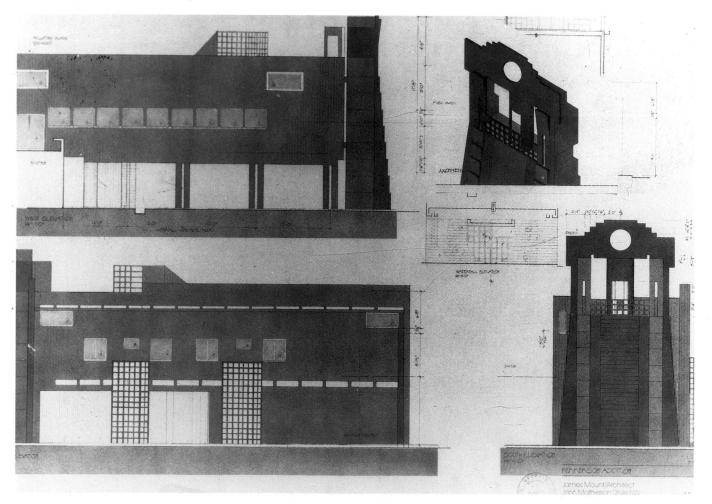

once the pyramids and pylons (the monumental gateways formed by towers and slanting walls) of Ancient Egypt, both somewhat grand and epic references for what is actually a more reduced, 1500-square-foot, single-family beach house in Florida. In contrast, the materials the architect has specified—plywood, particle board, galvanized metal, and glass—are modern applications. Their reduced geometries investigate form in the manner of more contemporary deconstructivists.

The house itself was designed as a series of sixteen-foot squares: Living, dining, and kitchen areas are squares that overlap, while two bedrooms are squares stacked upon one another. The rooftop area, the architect explains, works as "positive and negative spaces" that relate to these interior quadrants. Above the bedroom is the semicircular shape that echoes the ceiling of the master bedroom. Over the interior stairway is the pyramid form. And over the living areas is the "announcer" form that announces both the more restrained entry on the facade below, as well as the arrival of a startling new neighbor in this community of traditional beach cottages. Also, a skylight installed at the base of The Announcer

permits natural light into the living and dining areas below. On its sloped plywood facade, one-foot squares of particle board have been applied in a grid pattern.

While the geometry of the forms reflects the uncluttered lines of sun, sea, and sky, the palette specified by Mount also refers to that of the natural landscape—"the pure white sand that is rosy pink in the early morning light, white at noon, and yellow pink at sunset." It is a soft palette that makes for a sharp contrast to the strong blue shadows of the subtropical climate. The palette of exterior color, then, varies in its gradations of pale pinks, yellows, and grays that reflect the changes of color that wash the sand and dunes at different times throughout the day and seasons. "The shifts in color and shape," Mount observes, "occur as if the form was placed in water, and the changes are a physical occurrence."

But accidental, physical occurrences can be real as well as perceived. A heavy fog that rolled in during the painting caused the acrylic paint to slide down the facade of The Announcer. When the painters hosed the sloped facade, the blue gray paint ran down the one-foot squares, exposing the pink color beneath. The clients found the effect

in sync with the form, and chose not to repaint.

As Mount observed in the planning and construction of the The Announcer, color may be a more significant factor in rural rooftop additions than it is in urban rooftop additions. Indeed, how the hues of the natural landscape change over the seasons, along with how the daily and seasonal changes in the light affect the color of the landscape, is more at issue in rural architecture. The Seaside folly designed by London-based architect Leon Krier was originally painted a vibrant barn red, perhaps a familiar idiomatic hue for New England, but glaring and improbable in this Flori-

---

Left *The Announcer. Photograph courtesy of Timothy Hursley*

Below *The Announcer, working drawing*

da beach community. Repainted, it is now sheathed in creamy white clapboard.

For obvious reasons, rural houses don't aspire to or achieve the lofty heights of urban architecture. Ironically, then, Krier's house *does* capitalize on the height of its site, which is a mere fifteen feet above sea level on the Gulf of Mexico. Located on the highest point of the Florida town of Seaside, the house, working as a gateway to the village, achieves a sublime height—if not of physical altitude, then certainly of stylistic invention.

The temple/studio perched on the rooftop of this house is an example of what is inescapably a rooftop folly constructed not as an afterthought but as an integrated part of the whole building. And the whole building is admittedly derived from the conventions of resort vernacular; composed as a series of porches and loggias, the house relies on well-known building idioms of any seaside retreat.

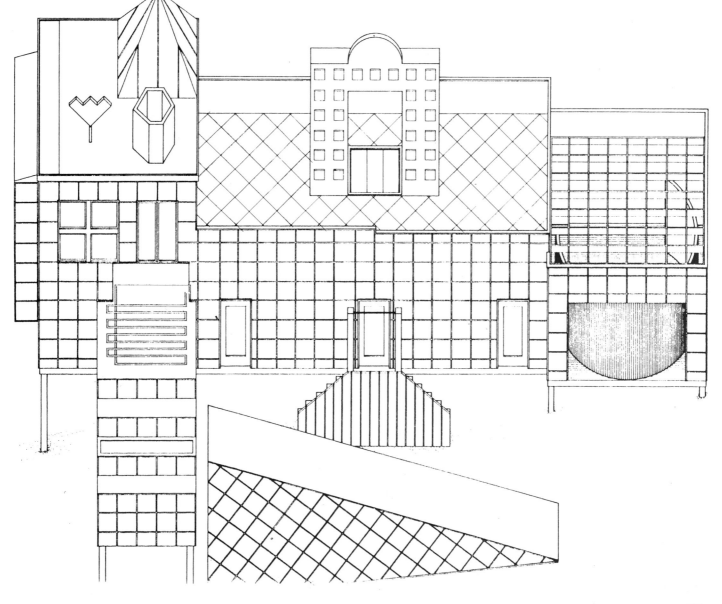

Not surprisingly, then, it is the view toward the south, toward the sea, that the house addresses most specifically—through the three windows of a second floor living room, and more dramatically, through the bowed window of the rooftop studio and the porch beyond. While the more distant view from the studio is of the Gulf, the immediate view is of the thicket of oak trees springing up beneath it. Here is a rooftop sanctuary, a fragment of a temple that is more connected with the textures of the natural world than with the community of other beach houses surrounding it.

That said, the studio is stylistically integrated with the building beneath it. A series of architectural details connect the different parts of the house—a criss-cross patterning is repeated in the various railings, for example, and the several column forms used throughout are all quiet deviations drawn from classical molds. The pitched roof of the studio reflects that of the second floor loggia. While the temple/studio may be the crowning achievement, literally and figuratively, it is not hard to think of the entire house as an exercise in architectural folly.

That Krier has achieved such a marvel of eccentricity in the planned community of Seaside is a small marvel of its own. All construction in the town is governed by the Seaside Development Group, which has established design guidelines with regard to materials, setbacks, and height. So in the end, what is at once curious and memorable about this folly is how the architect has used such familiar, indeed conventional, forms and materials to devise such a precise study of built eccentricity.

Rural rooftops have less need than their urban counterparts to serve as private sanctuaries. The landscape they occupy is already a private one, and if anything, these additions may even tend to make a more public statement; that is, they may be designed for public view. The design of rural rooftop additions is not governed by the same sense of distance from their immediate landscape. Their geography is not one of tiny cottages perched atop vast urban canyons; rather, they are constructed as a more integrated part of their immediate landscape, be it treetops, gardens, or sand dunes. Theirs is a relationship to the environment that is governed by intimacy rather than separation. Clearly, The Announcer and Krier's folly are intended to stand out in the rural landscape.

The rooftop of a house on upstate New York's Cayuga Lake designed by architects Simon Un-gers and Laszlo Kiss is not simply a marker of the country landscape: It serves more purposefully as a navigational device. Sailers on the nearby Cayuga Lake look to the pitched roofline to confirm their bearings.

The house could also serve as a stylistic directional device for future-thinking architects addressing the growing market for small, low cost homes. Constructed on a low budget, and tucked into a grassy hillside, the house has been built as a cube of concrete blocks containing a single room—measuring twenty-six by twenty-six feet—and a bath. And while its modest proportions, simple use of simple materials (concrete, wood, and glass), and graceful siting are enough to distinguish the house, it is the roofline that is its crowning achievement.

The structure is an eclectic mix of a formal entrance, garden pavilion, terrace, and aerie all at once. Indeed, one does not customarily enter a house from at the rooftop level. Nonetheless, a wide set of steps leads from the parking area to the rooftop. There, while the open structure of columns and beams suggests the frame of a house, it also composes a series of frames for the panoramic landscape that lies beyond. Another set of exterior stairs at one side of the house leads downhill to the actual entry of the house.

To augment the sense of interior space, the walls have been extended beyond the central, ten-foot-high ceilings and 2 1/2 feet above the supporting columns to create a gallerylike space that also accommodates indirect lighting. There, the owner of the house, a curator and professor of art history, can hang large canvases and wall hangings—an otherwise unlikely feat in a house of such reduced dimensions. This layering of space is directly reflected above where banquette seating runs along the periphery of the rooftop.

While these banquettes make for a neat fit with the interior architecture of the house, more to the point are the expansive views of the surrounding countryside and lake they afford. Broad vistas abound here: Although the scale of the house is certainly small, there is nothing downsized about the vision required to produce such a precise, perfect building.

Although these rural rooftops may investigate design directions that are governed by their rural site, some of their ideas may be applicable to urban rooftops as well. The format of a rooftop

frame used by Ungers and Kiss, Krier's temple/studio, and the geometrics of Mount's Announcer could all find urban translations. Indeed, as a design laboratory, the rooftop terrain encourages designers to work out such translations. And several conceptual projects indicate that the rooftop is a design laboratory that can function on paper almost as usefully as it does in the built world.

Numerous urban architects have looked to the rooftop for proposed additions. While these have yet to be built, their design inquiries and resolutions are final testimony to the rooftop as an inspiring and productive design lab. Consider the Tar Beach Pavilion, which used two watertowers as its point of departure. As Los Angeles architect Deborah Weintraub explains of the plan, "The existing watertower has a minimalist presence of some power and beauty. Its reduced forms, the strict rectilinearity of the overall mass, and the simple curves of the wooden water barrels suggested the basic vocabulary of the pavilion." In-

deed, the plan for the rooftop pavilion she designed with contractor/designer Ken Forman gracefully exploits the simple vocabulary of forms found on the rooftop.

Known as Tar Beach Pavilion, the project was to add a small enclosed addition and garden above a loft on the sixteenth floor of a warehouse building in New York City. The existing watertower and fire stairs suggested the vocabulary of simple, geometric forms; yet their simplicity does not detract from the very real functions they serve. In an effort to accommodate the four seasons "as any good garden pavilion should," the small indoor area has both a fireplace and a hot tub. Sliding doors permit the interior space to be opened up entirely in warm weather. Indeed, the purpose of the pavilion is to reacquaint the urban dweller with the eclectic nature of the urban outdoors: On the southern edge of the pavilion is a small court planted with deciduous trees; to the north, low plantings permit the Empire State Building to maintain its powerful presence.

A wall that has been painted hedge green on one side and water blue on the other separates pavilion and garden from the water towers; it also serves as a demarcation between living and service areas. Weintraub and Forman imagined the

---

Right *Pathway leading to the rooftop frame. Photograph courtesy of Karen Bussolini*

Left *Entrance to the rooftop frame. Photograph courtesy Karen Bussolini*

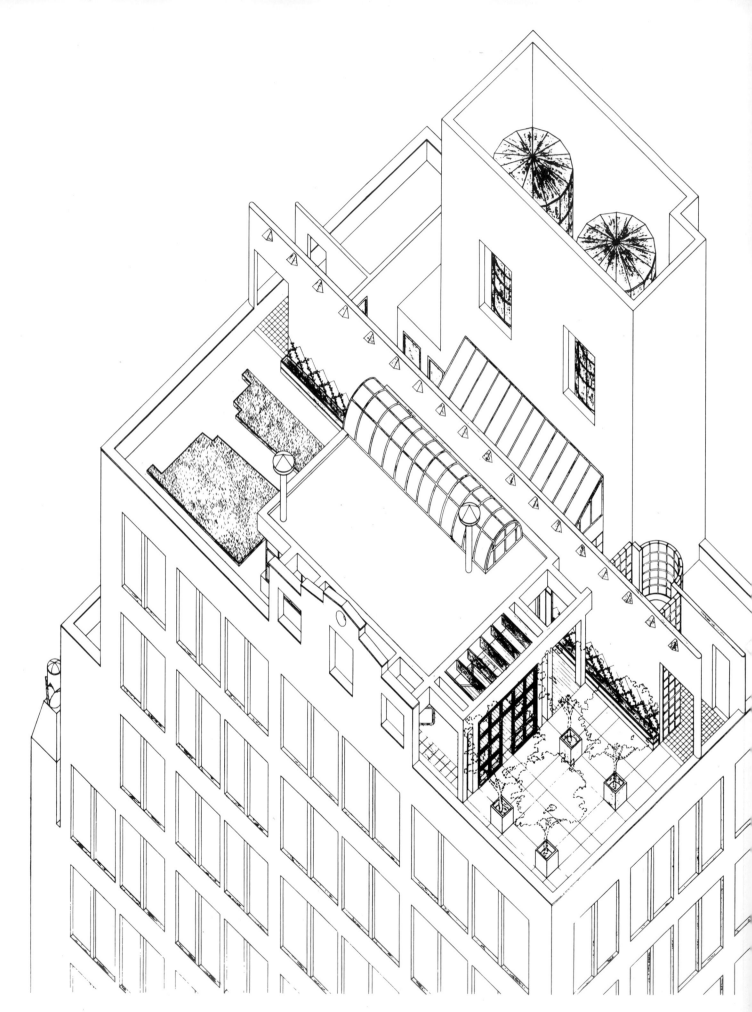

rooftop terrain as a plot of land, an approach to the urban outdoors that Weintraub attributes in part to time spent on the West Coast. Yet unbuilt, the Tar Beach Pavilion tests a formula for bringing together diverse elements of the urban environment: Sunlight, shade, vegetation, and wind are elements of design just as surely as the man-made grid, concrete, masonry, and blacktop are.

New York architect Lee Skolnick's rooftop plan for a six-story industrial warehouse, also in New York City, resides on an even more theoretical landscape. All the same, it acknowledges the various shifts in perception that rooftop building may induce—reversals in what is above and below ground and reversals in what is organic and man-made.

Traditionally, architecture is the business of installing a nonorganic structure in the organic environment. Here, however, the elevated ground-plane is a man-made landscape; in counterpoint to it are the organic constructs. Skolnick has used a tree and a hedge as rooted, naturalistic guideposts that orient the viewer in the man-made landscape.

The plan accounts as well for the approach to the roof, the vertical circulation below the "ground" surface. As the steel staircase from the street level approaches the roofline, its form changes from a parallel scissor-shape to that of a corkscrew, suggesting a gaining momentum. At the top of these stairs is a platform that leads to a steel bridge. By spanning the street below at an angle, the actual east-west orientation of the bridge points out the discrepancy between the artificial and man-made grid of the urban landscape and the natural polar axis of the earth. The bridge, positioned at the final point of the vertical procession, emphasizes the reorientation of the ground-plane by obscuring the view outward, and permitting only views up and down. Finally, at this terminus, is the tree, the "rooted guidepost." The irony, says the architect, is that the architecture

---

Left *Tar Beach Pavilion, axonometric drawing*

Below *Tar Beach Pavilion. interior view*

here is one of the site rather than what has been installed on it.

Architect Andrew Bartle of Architrope, also in New York City, has chosen the same site, the rooftops of New York City's Soho, for his Desert Pavilion. The dominant architecture in this particular area is that of light industrial, cast iron buildings, all virtually the same height. No sur-prise, then, that Bartle viewed the roofscape as a veritable desert of blacktop. The rooftop studio he subsequently designed for a painter—who had a fifth-floor loft and roof rights—was conceived as a Roman "tent," an exotic outpost that might disrupt the monotony of the asphalt dunes for the fortunate urban nomad.

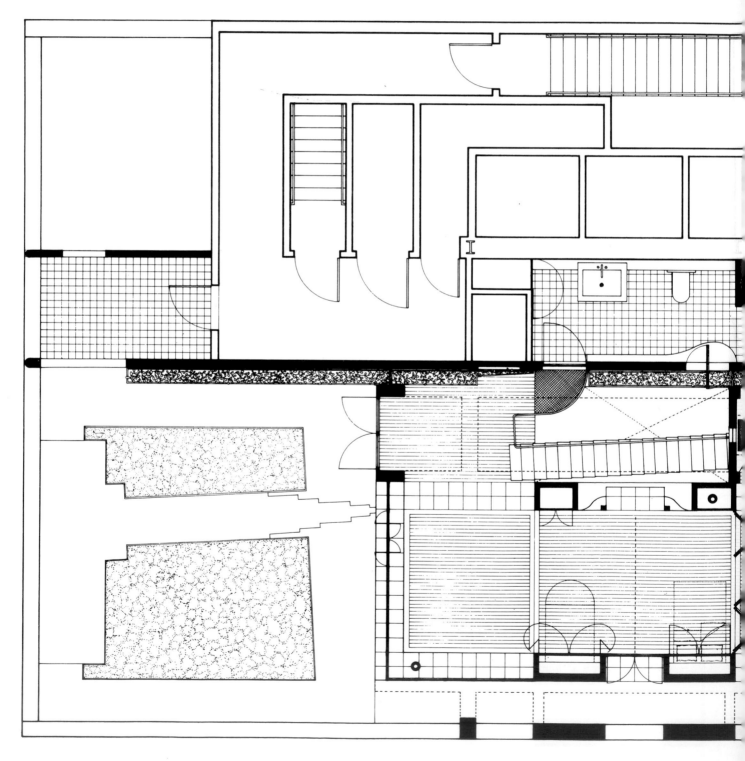

Below *Tar Beach Pavilion, floor plan*

Right *Tar Beach Pavilion, north elevation*

Right *Tar Beach Pavilion, south elevation*

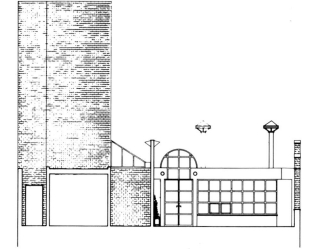

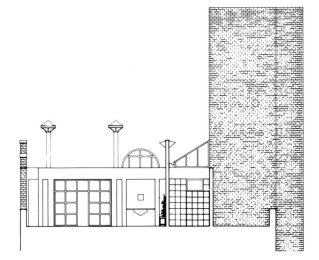

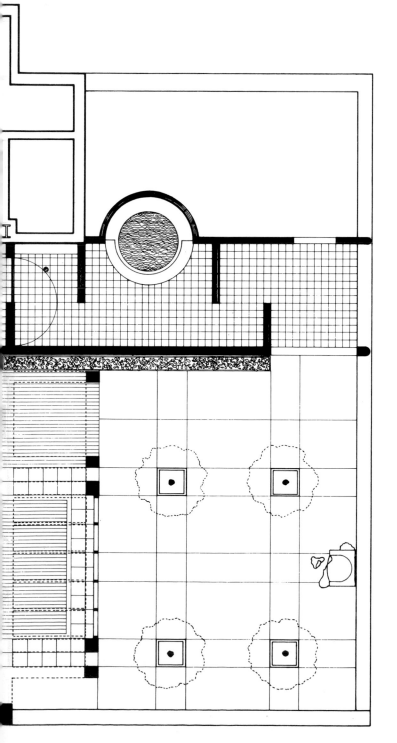

Because most of the buildings in this district are of a consistently low height, five to seven stories, Bartle specified materials that might exploit the abundance of available light. Roofing for the twenty-five square foot pavilion is a sheet of translucent fiberglass mesh stretched between eight fabricated steel trusses. Installed in the roof at an angle and in the form of spears, the trusses suggest that this is an impromptu pavilion. In fact, the construction was to be a more solid structure with masonry and tile walls. Even the mass of these walls, however, is broken by a transom of patterned glass that runs along the upper section. To bring light from the transom into the residence and printing studio below, the architect also specified a floor with sections of translucent glass blocks and an open interior staircase.

Unfortunately, the desert metaphor was all too accurate, and the pavilion remains unbuilt, a mirage for architect and client alike. At about the same time the addition was being designed, new zoning regulations in the area were enacted to prohibit the addition of floor area to existing buildings. All the same, the plans remain as a bright focal point, if not on the terrain of black-top, then on that of more conceptual landscape of urban design.

If the rooftop village is to further develop and to become that second city in the sky anticipated by some architects and developers, the profile of that city as yet remains vague and undefined. These proposals, some on paper and others taking physical shape in the rural landscape, suggest only some of the possible shapes it might take. What they also suggest, of course, is that the metropolis of the roofscape will be a diverse, often outlandish, but always animated and spirited landscape of design and ideas.

Right *Skolnick progression*

Below *Desert Pavilion*

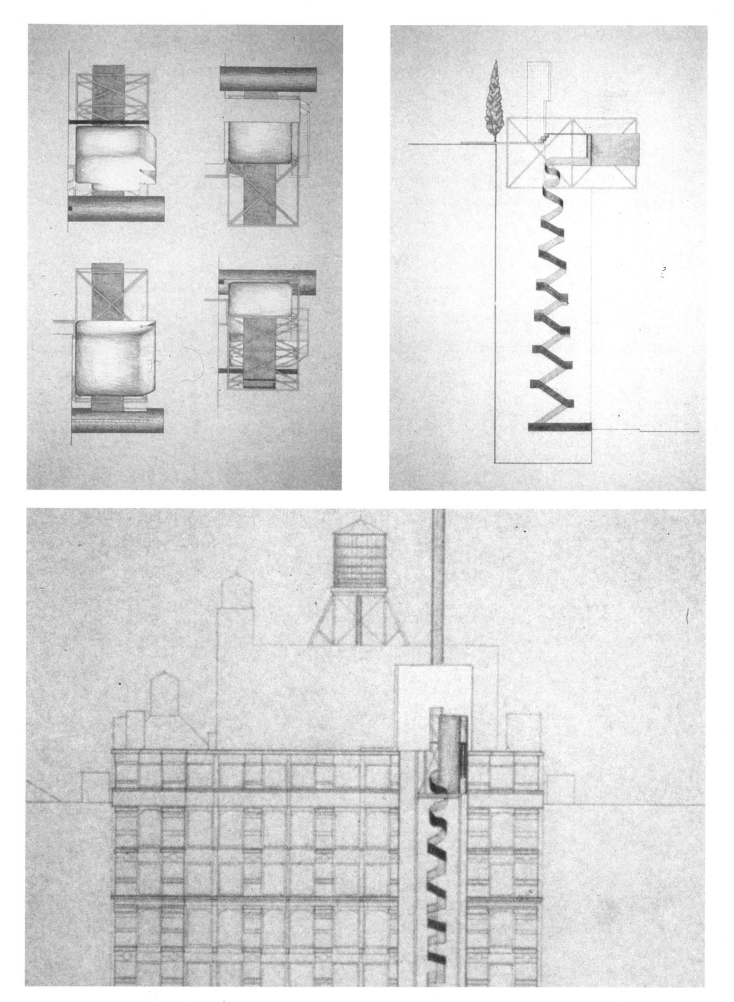

WHERE, WHEN, AND HOW TO GO IF YOU'RE GOING UP

New York architect Henry Smith-Miller likes to think of the rooftop as the fifth wall. "This is the benefit of living at the top," he observes. "Most apartments have two exposures. As you go higher in the building, you may get three, then four. And with four exposures, you become much more aware of the passage of the sun, the changes in the light throughout the day, and seasons. It's not unlike the awareness of nature you have living in the country. Your apartment works something like a clock. But if you're on the top floor of the building, the rooftop can work as a fifth wall. It's another surface you can poke holes in."

Working with this fifth wall, though, is a complex process. If the virgin acreage of the rooftop is extensive, so too are the construction and zoning variables, the legalities, and certainly the expense that come with building on it. While the specifics of all of these issues differ from city to city, most prospective rooftop dwellers will face at least some of them.

Perhaps the first issue the prospective rooftop tenant will face is the cost of building. Although this may not hold true for the future, the costs of rooftop construction are substantially higher than those of building on the ground. For now, the rooftop remains a zone of luxury living rather than a low-rent building lot. In New York City, for example, architects put the price of new building at approximately $150 per square foot for a custom residential project. Architect Jane Siris notes that for the rooftop, however, prices as well as construction go through the roof. Generally assuming that the cost of building on the roof is easily double that of building on the ground, she advises her clients to count on spending somewhere between $300 and $400 per square foot. In San Francisco, construction costs are somewhat lower. Architect Theodore Brown puts them at $125 per square foot for new construction at ground level and at $200 to $250 for rooftop construction.

Overleaf *Smith and Thompson rooftop addition, exterior construction shot*

The photograph here and those on the following pages illustrate the ongoing construction of a rooftop addition for a brownstone on Manhattan's Upper West Side. Designed by Smith and Thompson Architects, the addition accommodates a master bedroom suite with sleeping and sitting ares to the south and bath, exercise, and dressing areas under a skylight and to the north, or street, side. The addition itself was part of a larger renovation program in which the entire house was returned to its original, single-family use. The renovation included changing the location of the staircase, adding an elevator, and converting the cellar to a children's recreation area, a chauffeur's room, and a bar.

The consolation in such soaring cost estimates is, of course, that the larger the construction project is, the more cost-effective it will be. New York City architect Phillip Smith observes that if the rooftop addition is to be for a New York City brownstone that is itself undergoing complete renovation, the costs for the rooftop construction might be $200 or $250 per square foot.

If one is prepared for the cost of rooftop building, the next step might be to establish the question of roof rights— a tricky term that may need redefining from project to project. If the client owns the building outright, roof rights are obviously no problem. A more likely scenario is that the client will have to negotiate roof rights from a co-op board. In some cases, roof rights can be part of the original co-op purchase, and when the time comes to build, the number of additional co-op shares and the increase in monthly payments are negotiated. Situations in which roof rights have not been included in the initial plan and need to be defined and negotiated are, of course, more complex. Co-op members on lower floors are likely to be skeptical about the added stress of rooftop additions, not to mention the likelihood of leaks during the construction. They may also be concerned about the possible modifications of the building's services—wiring, plumbing, and drainage—when these are extended to the rooftop. Obviously, all of these concerns should be mediated well in advance of any construction.

On rooftops that are shared with other tenants of the building, prospective rooftop tenants might consider using existing residential space as a negotiating tool in obtaining more extensive roof rights. If the construction project is to include substantial interior demolition and rebuilding, using interior square footage might be a creative way to bargain for extra roof space. Although the help of an architect might facilitate these negotiations, for the most part they are actually carried out by the client or tenant.

Along with settling the question of roof rights, the tenant must also obviously determine whether the rooftop is a viable building lot. Determining the structural integrity of the building can be especially difficult if plans of the existing building are not available, as is often the case with older buildings. A structural engineer hired independently or through an architect can take on such a feasibility study to investigate whether the existing roof can support additional loads and if so, how much. Says Phillip Smith, "We always hire a consultant engineer to verify our own findings. It's like getting a second opinion—everyone benefits from it. As an architect, you're always trying to protect yourself, and this is one way to do it."

Smith also points out that it may be wise to document the condition of adjacent buildings. The mere presence of jack hammers and drills make some neighbors nervous, not to mention litigious, and long-standing cracks in the wall may suddenly seem much more visible. Brownstones, especially, may have party or shared walls with adjacent buildings, and the condition of these should always be documented with photographs before construction begins.

Feasibility studies will often conclude that the rooftop is incapable of supporting additional weight. The roof of a building, after all, is conventionally designed not to support a floor load but to carry the weight of rain or snow and only the occasional human visitor. But a finding that the roof cannot support the weight of an addition need not prohibit rooftop building. There are numerous other ways to support rooftop building. Henry Smith-Miller points out that in many city buildings, heavy elevator equipment, including the motor, are put on the rooftop, rather than in the basement where there may be excessive moisture. The rooftop may also have to support

the weight of a water tower. Dunnage, the construction term for the steel beams spanning the roof of the building, support the weight of this equipment. The dunnage itself is supported by the walls of the building, which in turn of course, are supported by the building's foundation. Situating the rooftop addition on top of the dunnage—especially if the addition is to be relatively small and constructed of lightweight materials such as corrugated metal or glass—may be one viable construction alternative. Again, the structural engineer can investigate the size and the condition of the dunnage.

Another possible alternative, if the rooftop itself is incapable of supporting additional weight, is to reinforce the construction from below, by having new floor joists supported by the building's load-bearing walls. Or, another method, feasible only for relatively low buildings, would be to drop new structural columns through the building onto the existing foundation and newly

---

Below Left *Smith and Thompson addition, exterior view*

Below *Smith and Thompson addition, exterior construction shot of skylight*

excavated footings. This is obviously an extensive and costly route that would only be demanded by a more substantial rooftop addition.

Once the question of roof rights has been settled and the structural integrity of the building and rooftop have been established, there are two sets of variables or restrictions that will apply to any new construction. The first are those of the local city's building department. These restrictions apply to such issues as egress; for example, in some cases, a rooftop addition is required to have two means of exit. The building department may also dictate construction materials. Its requirements will vary with building type. In New York City, for example, additions designed for brownstones can be constructed with wood-frame-and-joist construction. Proposals for additions for larger, higher-density residential apartment buildings, on the other hand, must specify the use of less flammable construction materials such as steel, concrete, or masonry. Additional fire safety requirements also need to be met. These are intended both to prevent fire and to contain

a fire in an isolated area, should one be started. The building department will also determine occupancy classifications, special uses, places of assembly, and load requirements that determine the weight a roof will support and the capability of any structure on the roof to withstand wind. (In considering the latter, shape, as well as weight, is a factor.)

Building permits are issued by the building department to ensure that what is built conforms to certain standards for safety. The permit is what permits building, and it must be obtained before new construction is undertaken; before alterations are made that will affect the foundation of the building; and before there is substantial demolition. In most cases, a building permit does not need to be obtained if new construction is to be a minor alteration or construction that might be considered repair work. Simple decks, terraces, and greenhouses that can be viewed as lightweight, temporary structures also may sometimes be constructed without a permit. The distinctions between these structures that require a permit and those that don't are, of course, critical, although shrewd architects conversant with local city codes can work with and around them. If zoning regulations, for example, prohibit adding floor

Below *Smith and Thompson addition, construction shot of barrel-vaulted ceiling*

space to an existing building, thereby making it impossible to obtain a building permit for a substantial rooftop addition, the addition could perhaps be modified or redesigned as a minor or temporary alteration.

Working with and around such distinctions is obviously a tricky affair, and if there is a question as to whether the proposed addition is a minor alteration or will demand more substantial construction, the question will, of course, be answered by the building department. Obviously, the architect's input is critical here, and the architect is also the one who generally handles the application to the department. If the clients or tenants want to handle the application themselves, they can certainly do so, as long as the plans have been stamped by a licensed architect or engineer.

The second set of restrictions are those of the zoning department. Obviously, these vary according to specific locations within urban areas. Most urban zoning is divided into residential, commercial, and manufacturing zoning districts, with each zone allowing different uses and mixed uses. Zoning restrictions that determine such factors as height, bulk, and setback vary from neighborhood to neighborhood. Floor area is one of the biggest issues.

Haus-Rucker Inc.'s pamphlet, *Rooftop Oasis Project: Tenant's Guide to Organizing a Rooftop Project* explains the objectives of the zoning department. (Although Haus-Rucker's guidelines refer specifically to New York City, these general remarks can have a broader application.)

> Zoning refers to the regulations of a building's use and height in specific areas of the city. Zoning laws were established to govern a building's effects on its surrounding environment—and the people in it—to avoid incompatible or conflicting circumstances . . . .
>
> If a proposal uses a rooftop as an extension of existing uses already permitted in the building, and the building's use within the zoning district is legal in the first place, there should be no zoning problem. The building code refers to this as "accessory use" and defines it as "a use or occupancy incidental to the principal use or occupancy of a building."

(Haus-Rucker Inc., *Rooftop Oasis Project: Tenant's Guide to Organizing a Rooftop Project,* edited by Caroll Michels, New York, 1976, p. 3)

Often, the proposed rooftop addition does not conform to the existing zoning regulations. New buildings, especially those built since the sixties, are usually constructed to the maximum permissible height and density. In such cases, an application can be made for a variance, an official permit from the city that allows the construction of such "exceptions." While getting a variance may certainly be worth the effort, it is probably also safe to assume that in most municipal bureaucracies, the effort will also be costly and time-consuming, thereby holding up the project for months and possibly even years. The builder or developer might in some cases be able to negotiate the purchase of air rights from neighboring buildings on the block that are underbuilt. Again, the time, frustration, and legal expense of such strategies may be impractical for a small residential project.

If the building happens to be in a landmark district, the plan will also have to be approved by the local municipal landmarks agency before a building permit can be approved. The chief concern of that agency is likely to be whether the aesthetics of the rooftop addition are consistent with those of the building and neighborhood; the underlying factor in these cases of course is the historical significance of the existing building. The landmarks agency is also likely to closely examine the setback of the addition—that is to say, to check whether it will be visible from the street—so sight-line diagrams would be submitted as part of the application. "The scale and massing of the new addition and whether it maintains the original proportions of the building will be especially scrutinized," says Phillip Smith. "They're [the landmarks agency is] not likely to approve a proposal for a building that overwhelms or intimidates the presence of the existing building."

In most cases, an addition proposed for a landmark district should be more in the nature of a rooftop accretion than a highly-designed structure that is intended to stand out. In some cases, however, landmarks groups have been known to prefer rooftop additions to more conventional additions, because there is less chance of the former being simply imitative of the original structure. Additions that try simply to continue or extend the design of the original building may be mistaken as part of the original design, and when this happens the addition may misrepresent or undermine what is original. Smith observes that in his experience, the landmarks agency "tends to respect an intelligent design with a new spirit of its own, rather than one that mimicked what was already there."

In some cities, such as San Francisco, there are also seismic considerations. Theodore Brown explains that in San Francisco, making a rooftop addition necessitates bringing the entire existing building up to code. This can require installing steel beams around the garage—if there is a garage; rebuilding or reinforcing the building's shear walls, the load-bearing walls that support the building; bolting down the entire structure more securely to the foundation; and, often, repairing and reinforcing the existing foundation. Obviously, these all add substantial and often discouraging costs, usually in the range of $20,000 to $100,000, to what was initially perceived as a simple rooftop addition. "People tend to be shocked at the amount of labor and construction that go into quake-proofing," he observes, but concludes that his clients have questioned it less since whole blocks of buildings in the Marina section of the city disastrously buckled in the earthquake that struck the city in October, 1989.

Once construction has been approved, there is the question of how to get building materials to the rooftop site. If the rooftop is relatively low, say three or four stories, an improvised scaffold-and-pulley system might be set up that could be operated by a three- or four-person construction crew. Such a sidewalk-hoist system has the benefit of being relatively easy to rig up and operate on an as-needed basis. Or, if the entire building is under construction, materials could be transported up through the gutted interior.

In some cases, too, the building's freight elevator or stairs can be used. Here, generosity and tact in human relations may facilitate the job: While the elevator itself may be available during posted hours, the actual hours the elevator operator is willing to work may be somewhat less defined. Indeed, many urban contractors admit to factoring in a substantial fee in their bids for a job—ranging anywhere from $50 for the entire duration of construction to $50 a week—which is to be slipped to members of the building's staff to ensure continued and expedient access to the "site."

Below *Smith and Thompson addition drawing*

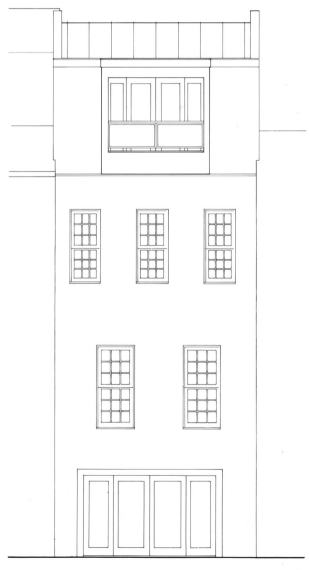

The obvious drawbacks to using stairs or elevators are the limited size and weight these facilities are designed to accommodate. Also, the service entrance to many buildings is often down a flight of narrow stairs or around a corner, or someplace with its own access problems. In some cases, too, the elevator doors—either at ground level, roof level, or both—may be too small to accommodate sheets of plywood or plasterboard, not to mention steel beams. Architects and contractors then need to ascertain whether it is more cost-effective to cut materials down to size and reassemble them at rooftop level, or to use the obvious alternative—a crane. Although the daily rental of a crane may seem exorbitant and the effort of getting a permit to operate it may seem laborious and frustrating, the cost of the labor demanded otherwise may in the end make it the most practical way to transport construction materials to the site. In most cases, this cost analysis will be included as part of the contracting bid.

Another factor to consider in getting materials to the roof is whether they need to be protect-

---

Below *Smith and Thompson addition, interior view of barrel-vaulted ceiling*

---

ed once they're there. Although it may seem expeditious to hire a crane and operator to lift building materials to the rooftop, if storing the materials on the roof—protecting them from both the ravages of climate and burglary—poses problems, the use of a crane may not be warranted.

Once the logistics of getting construction materials to the roof have been figured out, there still remains the question of when, precisely, to go through the roof. Can construction be done on the roof before the cut is made, assuring the installation of walls and a roof before exposing the building to the elements? Jane Siris states emphatically that "The last thing you want to do is to cut through the roof. You want your structure to be absolutely watertight before you do that. In our own residence, we didn't have the final siding in place [when we cut through], but the underlayment was in place and the windows installed. You want to be as finished as you can [be] before you make the cut."

All the same, if the cut is made before the construction is watertight, synthetic tents and tarpaulins can be rigged to protect the site. While Phillip Smith compares the effect of such tenting to

"some piece of artwork by Christo, only it's bright blue," he has found it effective—as well as aesthetically appealing. "Obviously," he says, "the whole thing is less of a problem if the whole building is under construction, but we've been able to work with a tarp until we've had the roof in place."

All of these considerations lead to the obvious conclusion that going through the roof also requires being insured. "Building on the rooftop," says Henry Smith-Miller, "is suit city, and architects planning on doing it should be well versed in exterior and renovation work. You have to be responsible for what's already there, as well as for what you're adding. It's a three-point strategy: You're dealing with the existing conditions, the modification of existing conditions, and your own new work."

The most obvious liabilities of rooftop building are the leaks that will inevitably be incurred sometime, somewhere during construction. Also, there is the obvious danger to the construction crew of working at such heights. Most co-op boards and building owners, however, require any contractors working on their property to carry a minimum coverage of liability, personal damage, and workmen's compensation insurance, and this usually will also cover rooftop construction. If a specific policy does need to be drawn up for the

Below *Smith and Thompson addition, elevation drawing*

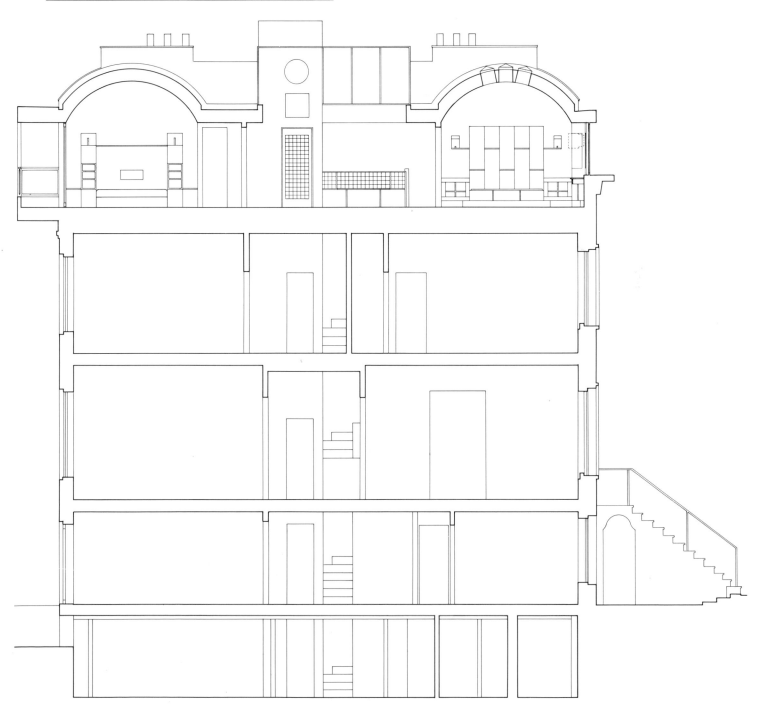

rooftop construction, a permit from the building department will facilitate it. The building department and the insurance supplier are both interested primarily in safeguarding the building and its occupants. Architects have been found to question the wisdom of carrying their own liability insurance, finding in some cases that the policy itself may generate the subsequent lawsuit.

The Haus-Rucker's *Tenant's Guide to Organizing a Rooftop Project* emphasizes the importance of carrying adequate insurance. The cautionary advice includes five points:

> In conclusion, be aware of the following points to protect yourself, your property and your investment: (1) Investigate insurance needs for your site early. Injuries and property damage can occur at any time, including during the construction period; (2) Learn what types of protection are currently in force for the roof and anyone on it. Some roofs may not need additional coverage; (3) The responsibility of risk should be clearly defined. Before the roof is used, the definition of risk should be legally established; (4) Consider liability and property damage coverage. Both types are significant and could prove to be essential if an unfortunate loss should occur; (5) Do not be dismayed if you find insurance coverage a difficulty. Insurance organizations for the most part have little or no underwriting experience for rooftops. Shop around for a receptive insurance agent. If the insurance organization is provided with sufficient information to underwrite the project, buying insurance should not be difficult.

(Haus-Rucker-Inc., *Rooftop Oasis Project: Tenant's Guide to Organizing a Rooftop Project,* edited by Caroll Michels, New York, 1976, p. 9)

The Haus-Rucker research team also itemized the following checklist of things for the prospective rooftop builder to consider:

A. **Scope of project**
1. Purpose of project
2. Project users
3. Special requirements of users
4. Is a building permit required

B. **Cost of materials**
1. Are they locally available
2. Are they available at a discount through tenants in the building
3. Must they be imported and how far
4. Expected life span versus cost
5. Ease of installation
6. Is fire-proofing necessary

C. **Professional services**
1. Architect
2. Engineer
3. Lawyer
4. Subcontractors such as carpenters, plumbers, electricians, roofers, special construction crew, riggers, and landscape architect.

D. **Maintenance**
1. General maintenance
   a. Normal cleaning
   b. Plant care
   c. Repairs
   d. Painting
   e. Who does it and how often

2. **Insurance**
   a. Liability
   b. Special policies
   c. Damage to roof
   d. Damage to floor below

E. **Taxes**—Who pays for the increase

F. **Miscellaneous**
1. Time and inflation rate
2. Quality of organization
3. Availability of materials and labor
4. Unforeseen setbacks
5. Adequate design planning

(Haus-Rucker-Inc., *Rooftop Oasis Project: Tenant's Guide to Organizing a Rooftop Project,* edited by Caroll Michels, New York, 1976, p. 14)

While such a checklist might suggest that the high cost, legal strategies, and complex construction maneuvers of rooftop building are daunting and extreme, homesteaders of the new urban frontier receive rewards that are perhaps equally extreme. The space, light, and virtual solitude of these urban aeries all attest to the fact that the rooftop may be the most valuable, yet most underused, space in the city. Those who have the financial and creative resources to pioneer this territory will find themselves stretching not only the limits of their imagination but the very limits of the conventional, earthbound urban landscape as well.

Additional Photo Credits:

p 18-19	Jane Siris
p 20	Ezra Stoller, copyright © ESTO
p 64-65	Elliott Kaufman
p 66	Imre Halasz
p 84-85	Michael Moran
p 86	Tim Street-Porter
p 110-111	© Peter Aaron/ESTO
p 112	© Peter Aaron/ESTO
p 134-5	Dick Busher
p 136	Hedrick-Blessing/Nick Merrick
p 152-3	Norman McGrath
p 154	Norman McGrath
p 166-7	Jane Lidz
p 168	Jane Lidz
p 176-7	Karen Bussolini

INDEX